THE ULTIMATE GUIDE TO RAID LOG

The only tool you need to run or rescue any project

Table of contents

This book is possible thanks to Madonna Swanson, one of the most amazing professionals I've had the pleasure to work with, who taught me what a RAID log is

This book is dedicated to all the project leaders out there who have the grit and determination to make things happen. I hope this book gives you one more tool to help you change the world.

PART 1: One project tool to rule them all: The RAID Log

"OK, I'll be there Monday and we'll see what we can do." I hung up the phone and took a deep breath, trying to wrap my head around what I just got myself into. Instead of a relaxing weekend at home, I was going to travel across the Atlantic, into the eye of a project shitstorm.

Though I lived in Phoenix, AZ, I had recently taken a position to build the Project Management organization for a UK based services company. In addition to the challenges of working across borders, building teams, and managing delivery, my new role also meant that I inherited the responsibility of putting out the project fires. And this first one was a raging inferno.

This project issue in the UK was scary, and had apparently been festering for weeks. It was so bad the customer issued a legal notice that, instead of paying for our troubled project, they intended to charge our company a huge penalty for the trouble we put them through. Not only would this be a big cost and the loss of a key customer, but it would also be an incredible blow to public confidence – just when we were trying to rebuild this organization.

By Monday morning I was sitting in a stuffy conference room somewhere in the UK midlands which smelled like old basements and cigarettes. I tried to shake off the jet lag as our infuriated customer berated us in the cold, cutting way only English wit can do. Every point they raised seemed frustratingly reasonable, and increasingly difficult to resolve. I looked to the team on my side of the conference table and they looked down in defeat as they took their verbal beating.

We had to turn this disaster around and we had less than one week to do it. The only tool I had? My RAID log. Before I share more about that adventure, let's talk about what a RAID log is.

Hello, RAID Log!

RAID logs are an indispensable tool, and anybody running a project, building a product, or running a team should be using one. In this book I will share with you what a RAID log is, how to build one to suit your needs, and several ways to use it – some of which will be new for even the most experienced project leaders. We'll also share some RAID limitations, how to definitely NOT use one, and a few best practices.

By the time you finish this book, you will be an expert with this most fundamental of project management tools. Few things build the confidence of your team, your stakeholders and yourself better than consistently demonstrating that you are on top of your projects, holding yourself and others accountable. This is what RAID logs do. If Batman were a project manager, he wouldn't need a utility belt. He would have a RAID belt!

This guide is for

I wrote this guide for different readers who can all benefit from the use of RAID Logs:

For Project Management Newbies...

This book will introduce you to RAID logs and help you learn how to use them so your projects can immediately benefit from better organization

For Experienced Project Leaders...

This book will provide innovative new ways to use your RAID log, some of which will definitely be new to you

For PMO and Portfolio Leaders...

This book will give you practical methods for mentoring your team and managing their delivery, as well as a method for providing better oversight of your portfolio

For Non-Project Managers...

This book will give you a free and easy tool you can use to run your team and all those little projects – even if you are not (officially) a project manager

For busy professionals...

We kept the length of this book down and added a lot of side bars, section titles and paragraph headers for readers who need to quickly find the information they need

> **Regardless of who you are, my goal in writing this book is to help you be a successful project leader by helping you master this fundamental project tool**

What this book is NOT

This book is not going to teach you everything you need to know about project management. What I am going to do is help you improve your management skills by giving you the most practical delivery tool imaginable, and give you pragmatic advice and examples for how to use it.

Not Just for "Projects"

In this book I'll refer to RAID logs in the context of a project because RAID was originally a project management tool. But it can just as easily be used to manage a product, a team, an initiative or any kind of change you are making. For all these purposes, a RAID log is just as useful as it is in a traditional project.

Who am I?

I'm a project manager, and definitely not a natural born one. I started off as a telephony engineer and moved into project management about 20 years ago. I was always attracted to tools and approaches that help solve the gritty real-world problems where things are not always like the textbook. And that describes this Ultimate Guide to RAID Log: practical, a little gritty and real world.

By the way, if you like this gritty and real world approach, check out my podcast, Project Management Happy Hour, which I do with one of my colleagues and favorite people, Kate Anderson. You can find us on your favorite podcast aggregators and at pmhappyhour.com.

How did my project rescue the UK turn out? We'll come back to that later in this book. But first, let's go deeper into how exactly RAID logs work

What is a RAID log for?

A RAID log is a simple but powerful tool for managing the delivery of work. The origins of RAID logs are lost to the dust of time; they were old-school 20+ years ago when I first learned about them. In my PM fantasies, I like to imagine Imhotep using a RAID log written in hieroglyphics when building pyramids in ancient Egypt. Whatever their origins, RAID logs continue to be incredibly useful not just because of their simplicity, but also because of their versatility.

RAID is a Tracking Tool

A RAID log is a simple tool used to track operational activities related to your project; specifically, Risks, Action items, Issues and Decisions. It is not the plan for the project, but instead it is everything you need to manage that plan to keep it on track. RAID logs were originally used by Project Managers but as we will see, they can offer value to other professionals as well.

RAID is a Methodology

Learning to use a RAID log will give you a method for being "always on" and up to date with your plans. It is a way of running your projects which can keep you focused on what is important and keep things moving, especially when you have multiple projects going on at once.

RAID is a Communication Tool

A RAID log helps you more clearly and efficiently communicate with your stakeholders and team members. As we will show later, the more challenging the environment, the more valuable your RAID log will become.

RAID is power in simplicity

Even though I will share some clever ways you can extend your RAID log, I encourage you to keep it as simple as possible. That's the power of the RAID log. The more chaotic the environment is, the more important it is to keep your RAID log a safe harbor of clarity and simplicity. Your RAID log should be light, easy to use, easy to understand and accessible. If you lose any of these characteristics, your RAID starts losing some value. You will be tempted to make it more complex, but don't. Keep it simple, keep it up to date and keep it accessible.

> The more chaotic the environment is, the more important it is to keep your RAID log a safe harbor of clarity and simplicity.

But a RAID is not…

A RAID log is not a replacement for good planning and sound project management, although it can help you to be better at both of those things.

A RAID log is primarily an operational tool, not a planning tool. It is a way to help you implement your plan and execute your project, but is typically not the plan itself. As the title of this book says, RAID is something you use to *run* your projects, or potentially to *rescue* projects that are in trouble. The actual detailed project plans or activity trackers are usually better served in a purpose-built scheduling or task management tool, rather than your RAID log.

That said, I have seen some people turn their RAID log into a Project Management super-system with a detailed schedule, budget, resource plan, everything - basically a portable Project and Portfolio Management tool for one project. This can work just fine in the right circumstances - it's quick and it's easy. But the greatest power in a RAID log is its simplicity, which you start to lose the bigger and more complex your RAID log gets.

PART 2: What is in a RAID log?

In its original and most simple form, a RAID log is a spreadsheet with four tabs; one each for tracking **R**isks, **A**ction items, **I**ssues, and **D**ecisions (R.A.I.D.) for a project. We'll talk more about how to use this log, how to extend it and other ways to host your RAID log throughout this book. But let's start with the basics of a RAID log: Risks, Action items, Issues and Decisions.

For each of the following RAID log tabs, we have included a list of recommended columns for building your own RAID log in the Appendix.

R = RISKS

No matter what industry you are in and what working methodology you use, the odds are against your success. Depending which report you look at, analysts find that as few as 31% of projects actually succeed in meeting all their goals. As many as 19% of all projects utterly fail, leaving the remaining 50% floundering somewhere in-between[1].

So, the question isn't whether or not things are going to go wrong with your project, but what are you going to do about them? That's why the first tab in your RAID log is the Risk tab. This is where we assess and plan responses for the risks that can affect the outcome of our projects.

Case Study: Risked if we do, risked if we don't.

For one project in particular, the wrong risk management approach could have landed me and my project team a segment on CNN.

My team and I were engaged to replace a very key piece of aging infrastructure for a global organization that depended on its massive supply chain to move

---

[1] CHAOS Report 2020, The Standish Group

millions of tons of material around the world every day. This particular piece of infrastructure was key for moving all that material - and it was reaching the end of its serviceable life. The clock was ticking to replace it before it failed.

But replacing this particular part of the infrastructure was very risky. So risky that if we got it wrong, we would take down the entire global enterprise. The supply chain would stop: airplanes wouldn't take off, materials wouldn't ship, and nobody in the enterprise would even be able to log into their computer. If that happened, my project would get a special mention on CNN that went something like, "Global organization X went down today, unable to move any materials through their supply chain due to a failed computer upgrade…"

Understandably, the organization was quite risk-averse, so we were going to recommend a very cautious approach, taking our time and building a process to carefully and gradually move each application and each service to the new infrastructure when it was good and ready. It could take a long time - maybe a year or more - but this was the safe way to go.

We were about to propose this "safe" approach when our customer's technical architect pulled us aside and said, "No, we can't do that. We should do a 'flash cut' and flip all applications and systems to the new infrastructure at once. One huge big-bang."

My project team was horrified at this idea. Flash cut the entire enterprise at once? Hundreds of business applications? Tens of thousands of devices and systems critical for keeping the supply chain moving? All at once? I could imagine our company name scrolling across the ticker at the bottom of the screen on CNN.

The technical architect's logic was that it was even more risky to let the organization gradually move over to the new infrastructure a little bit at a time. They tried that before with a similar bit of infrastructure, and 10 years later that migration still was not complete. With the clock ticking on the life of the infrastructure we were supporting, we didn't have 2 years to wait, let alone 10. In his view, the odds were that the migration would not be complete before it totally failed, creating a great many more issues than would happen if we went for a flash-cut.

So, what do we do? For this risk-averse organization, do we go for the long, slow insidious risk that will eventually catch up with the organization? Or do we rip off the bandaid and force the organization to make a conscious, if potentially traumatic, leap to a new infrastructure? There is risk either way, and the business had to make a well informed decision about how to proceed.

This is what enterprise risk management is all about. Before I tell you how that project went, let's talk more about risk.

What is a Risk in a RAID log?

A Risk is something that *could* go wrong with your project, *but has not gone wrong yet*. This is different from an Issue, which is something that has already gone wrong. Risk is about any uncertain event, so it could be something that goes unexpectedly well with your project which you want to take advantage of, or it could be something unexpectedly bad that you want to try to avoid. Things definitely seem to go unexpectedly wrong more often than unexpectedly well, so we will focus most of our discussion here on managing the down-side.

It's human nature to be averse to talking about risk. Most of us don't like to talk about death, even though we know it will eventually happen to everyone. Mahan Khalsa in his book, "Let's Get Real or Let's Not Play," compares this reluctance to address risk to yellow lights. When we drive and see a yellow light, most of us have an instinct to hit the gas and try to make it through. Project risks are the same.

Often, we can sense those yellow lights in our projects. We get that feeling that something is not quite right and we may be at risk. But too often we just put the pedal to the floor and hope we can make it through that intersection without a terrible accident. That may work a few times but eventually, at some point, it will catch up with us.

Why should I track Risks?

The idea behind logging risks is to consciously identify where your project can go wrong so you do something about it before it actually goes wrong. Risk management is pertinent for all projects, regardless of your way of working. Not only are you lying to yourself and your stakeholders if you pretend risks don't exist, but you are also setting your project up for failure. The best thing you can do for yourself, your team, your stakeholders, and your project is to manage risk from the outset.

> Things can go wrong in all projects. You are setting your team, yourself and your project up for failure if you don't plan for it.

Risk Culture

For risk management to really work, you need a culture where it is OK to talk openly about risk. In our risk case study, we had cultivated an environment where we could openly talk about risk at all levels, from the project team to our executive sponsors. This kind of open dialogue is something to strive for in your organization. But the reality is that many organizations are not comfortable talking about risk, which makes it very difficult to manage risk in your project.

If you are in a situation where discussing risk is controversial, don't let that stop you. If you are in charge of a project, talking about risk is part of your job: if you don't talk about the risks to your project, who will? You may end up spending nearly as much time educating your team, stakeholders and sponsors about risk as you do doing actual risk management, but you'll end up far better off than if you simply ignore risks because nobody wants to talk about them.

Appetite?

In thinking about your organization's cultural attitude toward risk, you will also want to understand their appetite for risk. Every organization has a different comfort level for risk taking, and that comfort will vary from project to project.

Some organizations will be totally OK with a "bull in a china shop" approach to push through a difficult change, happy to take a few lumps along the way so long as it gets the job done. And the same organization may have no tolerance for any kind of pain when it comes to a different project, where collateral damage may not be as easy to stomach.

So, before you begin thinking about individual risks for your project, establish first what the organization's appetite for risk is on your particular project. Then, take it a step further and identify how sensitive the organization is to different kinds of potential risk impacts such as financial impacts, schedule, scope & quality impacts.

An effective exercise I've used to clarify risk appetite is to create post-it notes with each of the following categories of risk impact, then work with my project sponsors and stakeholders to stack-rank them in order of importance. This will then guide prioritization of risks by their areas of impacts, which may include:

- Financial impacts (cost, cash flow, ROI, revenue)

- Schedule impacts (milestones, completion deadlines)

- Scope impacts (what must be in scope vs what can wait for later projects)

- Quality (how good is good enough?)

- Resource (team capacity, potential for over-work, internal vs contract labor)

- Operational impacts (impact to ongoing production or business operations)

You can take this exercise further by establishing the specific risk tolerances in each area. For example, when it comes to schedule impacts, discuss how much schedule delay could be tolerated without severely impacting the value expected from the project - and how much schedule delay it would take to make the project not worth doing.

Once you have a sound understanding of your organization's appetite for risk on your project, you are then ready to proceed with identification and analysis of specific risks. As you do so, ensure that the time and effort you spend in risk management is appropriate for your project. If your organization is sensitive to the risks your project brings, then you should expect to spend a large amount of time finding ways to avoid or mitigate those risks. If the stakes are not that high, then you should be prudent about the amount of time spent. But even with projects that are perceived as lower risk, you should still take some time to identify and analyze the bigger risks.

> Ensure that the time and effort you spend in risk management is appropriate for your project

Risk is Not an End in Itself

While a Risk log is an essential project tool, creating a long list of risks is not useful in itself. In fact, creating a Risk log is a complete waste of time if you don't actually do something with it. What happens far too often is that project managers log dozens and dozens of risks at the beginning of a project because that is what they were taught to do as a PM, and they stop there. They don't take action on them and seldom, if ever, look at the Risk log again. This is a mistake PMs everywhere make far too often, to the detriment of their projects.

Every risk you identify should result in one or more of the following actions:

1. **Respond by adjusting your project to reduce the likelihood of the risk happening or the impact if it does. Or, find a way to make it someone else's problem**

   Example: To manage the risk of materials arriving late, you can adjust your plan by placing your order early, looking for alternative suppliers, paying for expedited shipping or choosing different materials that are easier to acquire.

   Example: To make this problem someone else's responsibility, you tell your contractors that they are responsible for acquiring all the materials while also committing to a schedule. Now, it's the contractor's problem to make sure the materials arrive on time.

2. **Create a contingency plan to execute in case the risk actually happens**

   Example: In case your materials arrive late, you could have a plan ready for your team to perform other activities while waiting for the materials to arrive

3. **Deliberately accept that the risk can happen and simply leave it at that - provided that, with the risk, the project is still worth moving ahead with**

   Example: Late arriving materials may actually not be that impactful - in which case you could simply plan to communicate to your team if the materials do arrive late and adjust the schedule accordingly.

How to use your Risk Log

Among the items in our RAID log (Risks, Actions, Issues, Decisions), the process for managing risk can be the most involved. There is an entire professional discipline around risk management which we can draw from. This doesn't mean that risk is necessarily more important than other items in our RAID log, it just means that there are more tools available to us than most other aspects of RAID. In the following pages we'll walk through a typical risk management process that is largely aligned with the Project Management Institute's *Standard for Risk Management in Portfolios, Programs and Projects.*

Risk Identification and Analysis Process

1) Identify Risks in a "Problem / Impact" Statement

Risk identification can begin once you and your team have a clear understanding of your project and your organization's appetite for risk on that project. Start by working with your project team to collaboratively identify and categorize things that can go wrong with your project. This is not an exercise that you do on your own as project manager.

One approach is to get your team in a conference room or on a videoconference, and share a copy of your empty RAID log. Start by prompting my team with something like, "let's walk through the project, beginning to end, and identify all the ways this can go wrong." At this stage, coach your team to resist the urge to problem solve. Don't fill out any more columns in your RAID log than just a short description of the risk. Your goal is to freely brainstorm a list of what can potentially go wrong – big and small.

As you write down each risk, document them in a problem / impact statement, capturing the potential issue and how it would impact project parameters like cost, schedule, scope and quality - the impact categories we stack ranked in the previous section.

Some examples of problem / impact statements:

- The equipment might arrive late from the distributor, causing us to reschedule the installation contractors – incurring a $1,000 fee

- Our Florida training event is scheduled at the peak of hurricane season, so weather disruptions could reduce attendance or force us to reschedule the event, delaying the rollout of our new product

- To finish the project, the organization's capital investment committee has to approve the project budget for next fiscal year. If they do not approve the budget, then we will not have the funds required to finish the project and cannot complete the deliverables

Depending on the risk appetite of your organization, this process can be in-depth and take several workshops, or it may be performed at a high level and done in an hour or so. This is where your understanding of the project environment and your professional judgment will come into play.

You and your team also don't have to rely exclusively on your brainstorming. If your organization has RAID logs from past, similar projects, this can be a great source of material for not only understanding what can go wrong, but what risk response strategies worked and didn't work for those risks.

When you have your initial list of risks captured in a problem/impact statement, now it's time to organize them by category.

2) Categorize & Organize

The next step is to categorize your risks. This will make it easier to manage the rest of the process. How you categorize them depends on your particular situation and will vary by project. You may choose to organize them by who will be involved in responding to the risks (HR, architecture team, support desk, marketing), how they are caused (risks caused by weather, risks caused by customer behavior, risk caused by technology), or by the kind of impacts (legal and compliance related risks, health and safety risks, etc.). Use whatever categorization, or multiple categories, that make it easiest for you to manage your risks.

3) Risk Prioritization (Qualitative Analysis)

All risks are not equal and do not deserve the same level of attention. So, once we have a reasonably complete and categories list, it's time to prioritize them.

Prioritization makes it possible to identify which risks we want to invest time in, so the prioritization process itself should not require a great investment of time and effort. The most efficient method is to engage the expert judgment of your team and collaboratively score each risk. For best results, consider engaging subject matter experts and impacted teams from across your organization to gain better insights into the risks. For example, if you have risks which could impact your organization's Support Desk and end users, bring in leaders from your Support Desk to help analyze and prioritize those risks. This is another benefit of risk categorization we did in step 2, above.

This is a subjective assessment performed by you and our team, which is why it is sometimes called a Qualitative Assessment. This is a judgment based analysis, so we aren't bringing in a lot of science here. The end goal of this process is simply to prioritize the risks, so don't get too hung up on the details.

The scoring of your risks is done in two dimensions:

Probability
How likely is this
risk to actually happen?

Impact
If it does happen, how
bad will the impacts be?

Probability is pretty straightforward in that it is a measure of likelihood ranging from so remote that it is nearly impossible to so likely that it is a near certainty.

Assessing impact is a bit more involved because there are many potential dimensions to impact. For example, risks can impact your project in terms of:

- Budget – your costs go up

- Schedule – work gets delayed

- Scope – deliverables can't be done

- Quality – deliverables may not come out quite as well

- Resources – the team may not be available to support the project as required

But realized risks can also impact your organization's core business operations, well beyond the scope of your project including:

- Production operation – impacting the way the business operates and supports its customers

- Reputation/ PR – impacting the way the market views your organization

- Customer Relationship – impacting customer satisfaction, threatening future business opportunities

So, when assessing the potential impact of a risk, be sure to assess the total impact, not just one dimension of it, or from the exclusive view of its impact to the project.

Scoring

There are different methods for scoring Probability and Impact. Some organizations like to use percentage (% chance and % impact to budget and schedule). This provides two scales of 0-100, which are intuitive and allow for a large range of choices. Another common approach is to use a scale of 1-5 for Probability and Impact, 1 being low, 5 being high.

Whatever method you use, be sure to clearly define the scale so your scoring is consistent and understood by your team. Below are some examples for a 5 point scale of probability and impact with definition for each level. Although a 5 point scale is common, you should use a scale that is familiar to your organization if they have one. I've worked with scales of all types, including a descending scale of 1-4 (1 being the highest value) for a Fortune 50 organization. It was weird, but that is what they were used to.

Example Definitions for 5 Step Probability and Impact Scoring

Probability could be scored as:

0-10%	Very unlikely
10 - 49%	Unlikely
50/50%	50/50
51-75%	Likely
75%+	Very likely

Impact could be defined as:

Low	<10% impact to project schedule, budget or scope. Miss no major project success factors, no impact to business operation
Minor	10-20% impact to project budget, schedule or scope. Miss no major project success factors, no impact to business operations
Moderate	20-30% impact to project budget, schedule or scope. Possible impact to major project success factors. Minor impact to business operations
Significant	30-50% impact to project budget, schedule or scope. Significant impact to major success factors. Clear impact to business operations
Critical	50%+ impact to project budget, schedule or scope. Inability to achieve project success factors. Significant impact or outage to some business operations

Prioritizing using P*I

Once you have the Probability and Impact scored, then you multiply the two numbers and get a "P*I" score. This numerical value represents the priority of the risk, which you can use to stack-rank and prioritize your risks for the next steps.

Some organizations have standards around how to handle risks of different P*I scores. For example, I worked with an organization that had a policy that any risk of P*I of 16 or higher (based on a 5x5 scale) had to be reported weekly to the project sponsor.

Remember, this is just a qualitative analysis to help you better understand which risks to focus your attention on. The P&I score is not proof of anything in itself. It's just a way to help you be smarter about risk management.

Accounting for Different Impacts

Although not a part of typical scoring, it is important to account for the prioritized impact areas discovered earlier. For example, if you have a project that must be completed by a certain date, then risks with a potential schedule impact are going to be more important than risks that don't even if they have the same P*I score. But how do you handle this in your log?

The simple method is to add a column to your Risk log which lists impact areas so you can sort and filter by them. But, this doesn't change your P*I score, so it's not a true reflection of priority.

Another method I've worked with is a bit sophisticated for a basic RAID spreadsheet, but provides more accurate scoring. That is to weigh the P*I score based on which impact area is affected. You would do this by adding different weights to each impact area (Scope, Schedule, Budget, etc.) and incorporating this into your P*I score. This is more complicated than is needed for most projects, but is an option when you have some very sensitive risk areas to consider.

Trigger Date

A risk's trigger date is the date by which a risk will either become an issue, or it can no longer become an issue and therefore no longer presents a risk. For example, if you have a risk that materials may not arrive on the job site in time for certain work to be performed, the risk will either become an issue if the materials don't arrive on that date, or the materials arrive on time and there is no longer a risk. In this case, the delivery date is the trigger date.

There are different schools of thought around capturing trigger date. Some PMs only track trigger date when it can be tied to an event in the project schedule. Some capture it on all risks and if there is not a specific trigger date, then the trigger date is the end of the project. And some project managers don't bother with trigger date at all. Personally, I like to always capture a trigger date: the exercise forces a bit more consideration of each risk, and risks can then be filtered for those with impending trigger dates which may need attention.

4) OPTIONAL: Quantitative Analysis - Bring in the Science

What do you do when you come across risks that are so big and potentially devastating that they may warrant re-thinking your entire project? If this happens, then you may need to invest some effort into analyzing those risks to understand them better. This is called quantitative analysis.

Quantitative analysis is the process of putting real numbers to the probability and impact of a risk. This requires additional investigation and maybe some data sampling and detailed analysis using statistical modeling. This investigation can go so far as to become a project unto itself.

Doing so lets you:

- Compare the potential cost, schedule or performance impact of the risk with the expected ROI of the project to see if the project is worthwhile in its current form

- Justify investment in appropriate risk responses

- Determine risk contingencies

This level of analysis is typically only worth the effort for the most significant risks on very large projects. In mining projects, for example, it makes sense to take samples and perform statistical analysis to determine if it makes sense to mine in a certain location or not. For the vast majority of projects, this level of rigor is neither accessible nor necessary, so we won't explore it much further in this book. The closest most project managers will get to this process is Expected Monetary Value

(EMV) analysis, and even that technique is only worthwhile in some circumstances.

Expected Monetary Value (EMV)

Expected Monetary Value is a method of risk analysis which quantifies the financial impact of key risks, and calculates the net value of the risk by multiplying that financial impact by the percent probability that it could occur.

For example, if we have a risk with a 25% probability of occurrence which could result in a $100,000 cost impact to our project, the Expected Monetary Value of that risk is .25 x $100,000 = $25,000. If we have another risk with a 50% probability of a $30,000 impact, the EMV of that risk is $15,000. Put those together, and the EMV of the project's risk is $40,000 ($25,000 + $15,000).

If the net benefit of our project is expected to be $30,000 and the EMV of our risks is greater than that ($40,000) then we should be asking if this project is worth the potential risks, or at the very least, if we should have contingency funds available.

	% Probability of Occurrence	Financial Impact	EMV
Risk 1	25%	$100,000	$25,000
Risk 2	50%	$30,000	$15,000
Total EMV			$40,000

This value-driven way to look at risks is beyond the maturity of most organizations, so is not something most project managers will be able to effectively employ. It can be difficult to assign a monetary value to risks that you can defend, especially those that are harder to quantify such as loss in customer satisfaction or team member productivity. And when EMV is used, it is not done on every risk; only the biggest and most impactful. But, it is a good tool to pull out of your bag when you encounter risks that are so big that they may counteract the expected project benefits, or if you need to justify your contingency reserves.

The EMV method can be useful in speaking with executive sponsors about risk in financial terms they understand. But, don't let the math of probabilities limit your thinking. Regardless of its probability, if the impact of any one risk could cancel out the value expected of the project or make the sponsors rethink undertaking the project, pay that risk some special attention.

> **If the impact of any one risk would counteract the value expected of the project or make the sponsors rethink undertaking the project, pay that risk some special attention.**

5) Response Planning

Now that we've prioritized all our risks and performed a deeper analysis of the risks that could potentially have a major impact, we can start planning how to respond to them. PMI's Project Management Body of Knowledge offers succinct advice for keeping your risk responses pragmatic:

Project teams should consistently identify potential risk responses with the following characteristics in mind:

- *Appropriate and timely to the significance of the risk,*

- *Cost effective,*

- *Realistic within the project context,*

- *Agreed to by relevant stakeholders, and*

- *Owned by a responsible person[2]*

Like our other risk planning exercises, response planning should be performed with your project team members and relevant subject matter experts. Starting with

---

[2] Project Management Institute. (2017). A guide to the Project Management Body of Knowledge (PMBOK guide) (6th ed.). Project Management Institute.

the highest priority risks (per your P*I score), your goal is to determine how (or if) you will respond to each risk.

Risk responses typically fall into one of four categories:

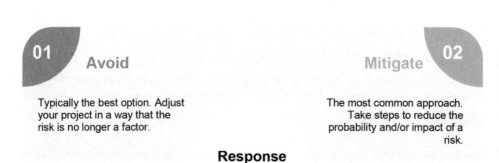

01 Avoid

Typically the best option. Adjust your project in a way that the risk is no longer a factor.

Mitigate 02

The most common approach. Take steps to reduce the probability and/or impact of a risk.

Response Strategy

Less common. Make the risk someone else's problem by transferring responsibility and the impacts to someone else.

Best for minor risks. Yeah, it could happen, so let's just budget some reserve in case it does.

Transfer

03

Accept

04

Whatever strategy your team selects, the resulting activities should feed back into your plan. This forms a loop where we identify and assess risks, determine our responses and adjust our plan accordingly, then repeat. Ideally, you will track the progress of those response tasks not just in your project plan or backlog, but also in your RAID log so you can see the status of the response activities in the context of each Risk.

Communicating the big ones

Although your RAID log should be transparent and available to your stakeholders, this isn't always enough. Sometimes you need to highlight a key risk and provide more detail than can be easily tracked in a RAID log. In these cases it can be a good idea to create a separate detailed Risk Report.

A Risk Report is simply a separate document which provides additional detail on the risk and the remediation plan. This additional focus on detail can help drive discussion and action around this one risk, and also provide a vehicle for your stakeholders and sponsors to communicate the risk higher in the organization when necessary.

Below is a simplified version of a Risk Report.

Residual risk - Optional

Once you determine the response plans for your risks, you can revisit the probability and impact for each risk, adjusting them to reflect new values considering the selected response strategies.

This can be an effective method for illustrating the effectiveness of your risk response. I once demonstrated to the CIO of a Fortune 50 enterprise the value of our team's proposal by plotting the probability and impact of their risks on a matrix, where the X axis was the probability and Y axis the impact. Of course there were many risks in the upper right with high probability and high impact. I then showed another matrix plotting the residual P&I after our proposed remediation steps – which moved nearly all risks down and to the left, with less probably and impact. The visual was so compelling that he engaged us immediately.

That said, for typical RAID management, it is more useful to keep the original P*I values, regardless of the response strategies. Doing so lets you prioritize the risk responses using the original Risk P*I score, keeping the response strategies for the most potentially impactful risks at the top of your list.

6) Communicate, Monitor, Reassess and Repeat

Now that you have your project plan updated to respond to risks, it's time to carry through and ensure those responses actually work as expected - or pivot and react if they don't. Run through at least the high priority risks on a regular (weekly) basis to ensure the response plans are on track.

It's during execution of your plan that **trigger dates** can be particularly useful. As a reminder, a trigger date is the date at which a risk either turns into a real issue, or the risk passes and becomes irrelevant. When you go through your regular risk reviews, pay attention to risks with trigger dates in the coming week(s).

And of course, you should not be doing this in isolation. As you execute your project and keep risks at front of mind, also ensure risk management is part of your

Consider Obstacles Instead of Risks

There is an interesting approach to risk management worth sharing from Dr. Josh Ramirez and his Institute for Neuro & Behavioral Project Management[3]. In many cases, it can be more useful to refer to risks as *obstacles*, rather than Risks. Cognitively, a Risk may or may not happen, so we fool ourselves into thinking we might get lucky and get away with ignoring it. This may be part of the reason it is hard to get ourselves and our teams actively engaged in risk management. On the other hand, conceptually, an *obstacle* is already in the way of success, so it must be dealt with and has more immediacy. As such, we may get more traction with our team and stakeholders if we refer to risks as obstacles - even if they are the same thing.

Using "obstacle" instead of "risk" can also have very practical repercussions. In some commercial situations, obstacles are handled differently contractually than risks, and may be eligible for more financial coverage.

Lessons from the Field: Ironman® race directors stay "1 hour ahead"

Far too often, Risk planning is done once, then ignored until it's too late. As long as your project is ongoing, you need to stay in front of the things that could go wrong.

I once had the opportunity to interview the race director for an Ironman® triathlon. On race day he is responsible for an event where as many as 3000 athletes push themselves to their physical limits over 140 miles of race course. As athletes progress through those 140 miles, he has to coordinate logistics for tons of food and water and thousands of volunteers to keep athletes safe and healthy. His method for keeping everything going smoothly was to "always think 1 hour ahead of the lead athlete." Focus on what needs to be ready next on the course, who needs to be there and what support needs to be in place to progress to the next milestone without issue.

This is a great way of thinking about risk, and one that all Project Managers should employ. The same way Ironman® race directors think an hour ahead of the lead athletes, PMs should be thinking a day, a week, maybe even a month ahead of

---

[3] https://www.nbpmi.com/

where their project is today, actively managing future activities and potential risks *before* you get to them.

Risks FAQ

Question	Answer
I work agile so we don't have risks. Why would I bother with risk management?	That's not what Agile means. Things can and do go wrong when using agile ways of working. Check out our chapter about Agile later in this book.
This is a lot of process around Risk! Do I really need to do all this stuff?	Not at all - the amount of effort you put into risk management should be a reflection of how much risk is in your project and your organization's risk tolerance. Scale your risk management activities to what makes sense for your project, but make sure you are doing something about risk.
Should I try to capture and analyze every single thing that could possibly go wrong? That's a lot!	This is where you and your team need to exercise some professional judgment. It's better to error on the side of capturing too many risks, but how detailed you get should be a reflection of how much risk your project has and the risk tolerance of your organization. Be thorough but don't go nuts.

Additional Risk Management resources

Check out the resources below for more information on risk management

- *A Guide to the Project Management Body of Knowledge (PMBOK Guide)* 6th Edition.

- Book: *Agile Risk Management* by Alan Moran. Springer, 2014.

Case Study Conclusion

Going back to the infrastructure project that gave us an opportunity to be on CNN, once we got over our shock at the architect's idea of doing a flash cut, we said,

"How about this - the Business needs to be OK with whichever way we go, since they ultimately bear the risks. Let's document the risks and our risk response plans for both options - going slow or going with a flash cut - and let them decide."

The architect was in full support of that, so we spent weeks documenting all the ways both approaches could go wrong and impact business operations, and developing plans to avoid or mitigate those risks. Finally, we presented them to a steering committee made up of executives from every major line of business in the organization. We were confident that this risk-averse organization would balk at the idea of a flash cut. When we finished the presentation, they said, "You've done a good job of thinking through the risks here. We feel good with the flash-cut approach. Go for it."

We were stunned at the decision, and, with some trepidation, moved ahead with the project. To help ensure our success, we implemented the most rigorous risk management process I've ever had in any project - an independent risk board supported by an outside risk coordinator to keep us honest with our risk management plans and activities. Several months later we flipped the switch on our global flash cut, flipping over hundreds of applications and thousands of devices which were used by hundreds of thousands of employees. And not a single thing went wrong. Best of all, we were not on the nightly news.

A = Actions

So many things to do! Even though we spend a lot of time and effort putting together detailed activity plans or backlogs & sprints for our project, other tasks never stop coming up; action items from meetings, little to-do's that have to get done, reminders to follow-up with other team members, tracking delegated tasks. How on earth can we keep it all straight?

Action Items and Trust Bricks

What's interesting about project teams is that they are temporary. Team members often go in not knowing each other and may never work with each other again afterward. Yet we depend on these temporary organizations to trust and work with each other effectively to build our entire world.

Further, these project teams often consist of individuals who have no pre-existing relationship. And if they do, it's not necessarily a good one. In a sense, most projects are like your least favorite group project back at school. You are thrust into a situation with strangers that you somehow have to find a way to work with or you are all going to fail.

So how do you do that? How do you quickly build working relationships with total strangers? One method I've developed and often speak about is the **trust brick**.

Visualize your relationship with another person as a bridge, made up of bricks. If you build your bridge with hundreds of interlocked bricks, your bridge is strong. It can even withstand having a few bricks break. On the other hand, if you build a bridge with one or two bricks and those bricks fail - the entire bridge falls down.

Trust bricks are interpersonal transactions which build a *bridge of trust*. You make a trust brick when you set an expectation, then meet that expectation. You say you're going to do something, then you do it, over and over again. Over time, this sets up the expectation - the cognitive bias - that when you say you're going to do something, we expect that you're going to do it. This is a very real and *resilient* kind of trust which you can intentionally develop and maintain. And like our bridge made of many trust bricks, when you make a mistake and break a few bricks - as we all do - our working relationship won't fall down.

And one tool we use to build those trust bricks? The Action Item log. Consistently following up on every commitment, every time is key to building trust.

What is an Action Item in a RAID log?

There are always tasks which come up *about* your plan which don't really belong *in* your plan. And as a project leader, it can sometimes feel like you have more to-do items outside your project plan than you have activities in the plan. So, a little organization can go a long way with these items. This is what your Action Items log is for. It's the daily to-do list for your project and by extension, you as project lead. There is not a lot more to it than that - the Action Item list is just your massive ongoing project to-do list.

Some examples of RAID Action items

Types of Action Items	Examples
Meeting Follow-ups	• Remind the VP that they need to send out the project announcement • Schedule a follow-up meeting to discuss a topic further
Team Logistics & Support	• Getting a list of all the company holidays observed by the team so you can update the project schedule • Open a support ticket for Facilities to fix your conference room projector
Project Support Activities	• Get the Project cost codes from your organization's finance department • Make sure the Change Order gets signed off by Finance • Get a copy of the organization's InfoSec policy

Why should I track Action Items?

If we track our Action Items in our RAID Log, does that mean it's a good idea to put all of the project plan tasks in a RAID Log, too? You could, but I think it's better to differentiate between Action Items and Project Activities and to track them separately.

Action Items NOT = Project Activities

Although Action Items and project activities are both things that need to get done, they are inherently different, so should be tracked and managed differently. Whether you use a Work Breakdown Structure (WBS) and detailed schedule or an agile backlog and sprints, project activities are focused on achieving the deliverables of the project. They have been accepted by the team, your sponsor, stakeholders or product owner as a planned part of the project and are usually built into a schedule or sprint and have budget and resource associated with them. As such, they should be under some level of change control.

Action Items, on the other hand, come up frequently and are much 'lighter' in nature than project activities. They don't have a direct impact on project deliverables but help support the efficient delivery of the project.

Deciding whether an activity is an Action Item in your RAID log or a project activity in your plan is a judgment call. But generally, if it meets any of the following criteria, it should go into your plan rather than the Action Item list.

An activity should go in your Project Plan rather than your RAID Action Item list if:

- If it produces a project deliverable, it goes in the plan

- If it is on critical path and impacts the schedule, it goes in the plan

- If it's important enough to track on a status report, goes in the plan

- if it has cost or "story points" associated with it, it should be in the plan.

- If it has predecessors and successors, it should be in the plan.

- If it can be done right now, it doesn't go in the plan.

...then it is probably a project activity and shouldn't be tracked in your RAID log Action Items.

How do I use my Action Item Log?

Capturing action items not only helps you stay organized, but can also help you stay more focused and productive. Putting actions down in writing frees up your mind to focus on other things, rather than trying to remember all the tasks you need to do. So, whether they are action items from meetings, inbound emails, or just random things that pop into your head, make sure you take note of them to free up your mental "RAM."

Action Item Basics

As you capture action items, make a habit of capturing not only the action item itself, but also who is responsible for doing it and when it will be done. Always be *that* project manager who insists on putting someone's name by each task and getting the assigned person to commit to a date for completion or an update.

- To follow up by email, filter your Action Items by the person assigned then copy and paste all assigned tasks into a follow-up email to that person. Do this once per week.

- To follow up in person, filter your log by people you are meeting with and, while you have their attention in the meeting, run through their list of actions and update them real-time.

As practice, if you think you can delegate a task, then you probably should. Knowing that you have a reliable way to follow-up can give you the confidence to do so.

Productivity Methodologies

There are a lot of methodologies out there for productivity, personal organization and task management. As you develop as a manager, it is worth investigating some of these approaches to develop your own method which works for you and incorporate into the way you mange your Action Items. A couple simple methods that I find useful are time-blocking and time-boxing.

- **Time-blocking** is simply allocating a block of time during your week (or maybe each day) to focus on action items. During this small block of time (30 minutes max), focus only on maintaining your action item list by completing them or follow-ing up on assigned items.

- **Time-boxing** is the technique of ruthlessly putting an age limit on your action items. Any item assigned to you which has been stagnant for 2 weeks should be either delegated to someone else or marked as "Indefinitely deferred" and closed. There are exceptions of course, but putting a limit on the age of items helps keep your action items from being a repository of low priority items that you will never do.

Action Item FAQ

Question	Answer
Why shouldn't I just put my RAID Action items into my project schedule or my backlog?	As project leaders, we get a lot of Action Items to deal with that don't directly contribute to project deliverables. If we put all the Action Items into the plan, it clouds the picture and makes it harder to see which activities directly contribute to project deliverables. Keeping Action Items separate lets you keep your plans and schedules focused on activities that directly achieve your project objectives
Why not just track my Action Items in a dedicated task management application?	You could, but that introduces task switching which is known to affect productivity. Your Action items are very often related to your other RAID items (risks, issues and decisions) so splitting that up makes your use of a RAID log less efficient.

Additional Task management Resources

• Book: *Getting Things Done* by David Allen. Penguin Books, 2017.

Trust Bricks Conclusion

Remember that every interaction, every committed action item and follow-up you have with a team member, stakeholder or sponsor, is either building trust or tearing it down, one brick (or action item) at a time. So, the next time you find yourself a part of a team, stop and ask yourself: Which am I doing? Am I building trust, or am I tearing it down? Make sure you are using your Action Item log to build those bricks.

I = Issues

For the most part, the only projects where nothing has gone wrong are those that haven't started yet. And even then, a surprisingly high number of projects are already in trouble. Despite our best intentions, our best planning and efforts, things go wrong with our projects. When things do go wrong, how you manage those issues will mean the difference not just between project failure and success, but also the personal success or failure of your team, yourself and your organization..

As the project leader, managing project issues is your job, and one of your most important responsibilities. It certainly can be the most stressful. So, you need to get it right the first time, every time. This is why you need an Issue Log.

Case Study: Managing Issues from a Fishbowl

I ran a project once where we implemented a new call center phone system for the IT help desk of a very large financial institution. Every call for tech support from the organization's 250,000 employees came in through this call center and was distributed to a hundred or so call center agents. Early the morning of go-live, everything was going well - our sponsors and stakeholders were excited and happy, there was a donut party, agents were happy with the new tools we gave them which promised to make their lives easier. We sat in a glass-walled 'fish-bowl' conference room in the center of the call center floor and everyone waved and gave us the thumbs up as the day got off to a fantastic start. Everything was great! Then it wasn't.

A couple hours into our morning, every light on our system monitoring dashboard went red. For some reason, every phone line froze up and not a single call from the entire organization could make it through our system to the call center agents, who now all started to stand up from their desks and look at us questioningly through the glass-walled fishbowl conference room.

As my engineer frantically tried to diagnose the problem and get the system back up, a half dozen stakeholders with titles of VP and above rounded the corner and started marching toward our fishbowl. They were not giving me a thumbs up. They burst into the room and demanded to know, "What the hell is going on? Why is our call center down?"

What is an Issue in a RAID log?

Whereas Risks are the things that *could* go wrong in your project, Issues are things that *have* gone wrong. Issues are not just the big problems that come up, but also all the small problems that cause deviations from your plan. As we'll see, Issues are usually the most urgent and sensitive RAID items when it comes to communication.

Why should I track Issues?

We track issues with three main purposes in mind:

01
To identify, communicate, and resolve issues as quickly and efficiently as possible

02
To learn from our issues so we can hopefully avoid them in the future

03
To provide a historical record of where things did not go as expected so we can explain any deviations in our project from the original plan

The Issue Log should be used to track everything that happened (or is happening) which did not go to plan and subsequently impacted the project. Obviously, big issues like system outages or non-performance to contract are things we would log as issues. But we should also track any event which forces us to change our project plan or deliverables. For example, if your customer is a couple days late providing a dependency, if your architect was out sick and had to push a key deliverable, or if the currency exchange rate fluctuates and now some materials cost more than budgeted – these are all issues you should log. The way to think of it is this: when the project is done, the Issue log should explain every unexpected difference between the approved project baseline (scope, schedule and budget) with the approved changes, and what was actually delivered.

When you review your RAID, your issue review should be first, focusing on active, in-flight (or on-fire!) issues.

Issue Sensitivity

If your team is not used to the concept of issue tracking and communication, documenting an issue can make some people very uncomfortable. This can be particularly true if you have to identify a person or team as part of the issue.

This is where your skills as a leader and communicator will come into play. On the one hand, you have to document the issue and hold team members accountable. But on the other hand, calling people out, especially your own team members, can impact morale if not done correctly. Even with the best intentions, when issues are communicated outside the project team, they can be misinterpreted and seen negatively, rather than as an opportunity for improvement. This can lead to negative opinions by external stakeholders who don't understand the whole story, and can damage trust in your project team.

For this reason some organizations, often those that are agile-leaning, prefer to keep issues internal to the team. The logic is that this fosters more open discussion of issues among the team members because there isn't fear of their dirty laundry being aired to external stakeholders. While team members do need to feel safe about confronting issues, the RAID log owner needs to be able to communicate issues to stakeholders outside the team when appropriate. The RAID log owner should work with the team to establish expectations on what is communicated outside the team and what is not. In your RAID log you can add a column to identify "internal" items which stay within the project delivery team, versus "external" items that are shared with external stakeholders. As project leader you need to have the final word on this, but being transparent about this to your team can help build trust.

Taking this concept a step further, there may be issues you need to record which shouldn't even be shared with your own team. For example, if there is a personality conflict between team members which is impacting morale and productivity, you might not want that Issue visible to internal members of the team, but you may need to escalate to specific members of your management team for advice and support. So, as project leaders, we need to exercise judgment for what we share and how we share it in our RAID log.

Whether they be internal only, external or "for my eyes only," you should find a way to document your issues, regardless. You need an honest log of the issues, and you will be remiss if you don't communicate issues that affect stakeholders to them. You will also be remiss if you don't identify internal team issues and don't have honest conversations to address them. But to safeguard sensitive issues, your RAID log platform needs a reliable way to protect access to sensitive Issues.

How do I use my Issue Log?

More than just a place to log things that went wrong, your Issue log provides you with a mechanism for communicating, resolving, remediating and learning from issues that occur on your project. That process may look like this:

1. Identify the issue

As soon as you have established that there is (or may be) an issue affecting your project, put it in your Issue log. Your understanding of the issue will grow over time, but first thing is to put it in your log so you can start collecting information to understand if there really is an issue, and how big the impact is.

2. Clarify the Impacts and the affected

Work with your team to get a comprehensive understanding of the issue's impacts not only to your project, but also to the broader organization affected by your project. Identify currently known impacts, potential impacts and all stakeholders who are or could be affected. This is the stage where, with the help of your team, you determine if there is a real issue, how bad it is, and how urgently you need to communicate and escalate it.

3. Communicate!

Now it's time to start communicating. Communicate the issue to the impacted stakeholders and your management team as appropriate. Be sure to be very clear about the issue, including what you know, what you do not know, and what the next steps are.

For critical ongoing issues especially, communication is key. When there is a critical issue, your team, your stakeholders and even your leadership team need direction and confidence that the issue will be resolved. Even if it is not possible to know exactly what the issue is or when it will be resolved, you can start building that confidence through good communication. This is where you as a PM can really shine if you rise to the occasion. One way to do so is by committing to a regular cadence. For example, "I will have an update for you in 30 minutes. That update may be that I have no news yet, but I will give you an update in 30 minutes regardless of our progress."

Although your stakeholders would prefer to have the issue is resolved, it's surprising how much peace of mind your stakeholders will have - and how much more space they will give you to resolve the issue - if you can give them something to have confidence in, even if that something else is simply that there will be a call in 30 minutes with an update.

Perhaps most importantly, don't communicate based on assumptions. Be transparent and be factual. It's better to say that you don't know than to make an assumption and give incorrect information. This can lead to finger-pointing and affixing blame incorrectly, potentially harming your team's credibility and damaging relationships.

There is a reason why communicating an issue is not the first thing you do. You need to first understand what the issue is, what the impacts are and to whom, otherwise you risk becoming the PM who cried wolf, escalating non-issues and losing stakeholder credibility.

4. Resolve and Remediate

It's OK not to have a resolution immediately, but you must have a plan to get to a resolution. As you develop and implement your plan to get to a resolution, capture the plan, activities and progress in your Issue log. Your Issue log should be the source of record for your resolution plan and progress, and is the ultimate tool for communicating progress to your stakeholders.

> **It's OK not to have a resolution immediately, but you must have a plan to get to a resolution.**

When it comes to solving issues, make sure you are clear about two categories of activities: resolution and remediation.

- **Resolution** is fixing the problem. For example, you have a broken pipe in your data center. This is resolved when the pipe is fixed and it is no longer leaking.

- **Remediation** is the cleanup after the fact - mopping up the water, replacing any damaged equipment and getting everything back into working order

It is important to understand the differences because remediation should typically be deferred until the issue is resolved and is no longer causing problems. In this example, there is limited value in mopping up the water until you've at least turned the water off.

Further, it can be easy to declare victory over an issue when a resolution has been found, but depending on the issue, resolution may be only a small part of setting things right. For many issues, there is a lot more to the unplanned remediation work to clean up after an issue than there was in resolving it. And avoiding or skimping on that remediation can cause yet more issues.

5. Root cause and Lesson Learned

Sometimes the root cause of an issue may seem readily apparent when you resolve it, but often it is not. If the root cause of an issue is not identified and you have no idea what caused it, there is risk that the issue may occur again. Establishing root cause is not always necessary for minor and obvious issues. But they should certainly be investigated for issues that are highly impactful, and the root cause addressed as well.

Even when the root cause seems obvious, dig deeper by asking "why" until you get to a satisfactory and addressable root cause. Something like the 5 Why's. Taking our broken water pipe example through this process:

Why did we flood?

A water pipe broke in our data center, causing the flood.

Why did it break?

One of the fittings failed

Why did it fail?

The fitting was not installed correctly

Why wasn't it installed correctly?

The plumber wasn't trained for this kind of plumbing installation

Why did we have a plumber that wasn't properly trained?

Because we don't have any method for vetting the quality of our suppliers or checking the quality of their work

The obvious bigger question would be why we had water plumbed near our data center in the first place, but the lesson here is not about plumbing, it's that drilling down into the root cause of impactful issues is essential for lessons learned - not just for your current project, but for future projects as well.

Converting Risks to Issues

Ideally, your Risk Management is so amazing that most issues that occur on your project were foreseen through the risk management process and you already have a response plan ready. This of course is not always the case, but when it is, you need a method to 'convert' a Risk in your Risk log to an Issue in your Issue log. When using a spreadsheet for your RAID, this is typically accomplished by copying and pasting from the Risk log to the Issue tab. In more sophisticated RAID platforms there may be automation which simplifies the process for you. However you do it, you need to move actualized Risks over to the Issue log because they are managed differently.

Risk + Issue on the Same Tab?

On some spreadsheet based RAID logs, you may see Risks and Issues tracked on the same spreadsheet tab to simplify the process of converting a Risk to an Issue. Although this may simplify administration a bit, it also causes confusion in the differentiation between a Risk and an Issue. I have actually had conversations with senior project leaders in three different organizations who thought that risks and issues were the same thing because they were on the same tab of their RAID log template. Risks and issues are of course very different, so to avoid confusion I recommend always tracking and managing them separately.

Lessons Learned review of Issues

Ideally, we want to learn from our experiences. This is where Issue logs can provide long term value to your organization. Every issue is an opportunity to learn and improve your planning, leadership and your organization.

You can take lessons learned from your issues as you manage them by creating a separate column to identify the lessons to be learned from each issue. Alternatively (or in addition), you can perform a formal issue review at the end of the project, analyzing all the issues your project encountered and identifying what can be improved for next time.

Case Study Conclusion: Surviving the Fishbowl

Meanwhile, back in our fishbowl, my customer executive stakeholders were waiting for an answer. "What is going on?! Why is our call center down?"

I remember looking over at my lead engineer who typed furiously on his laptop trying to diagnose the problem, afraid to look up in case he'd be asked a question he couldn't answer.

I took a deep breath and looked my stakeholders in the eyes. "The system is down and no inbound calls are being received. Ongoing calls have not been disconnected but no new calls can come in. We recommend performing a 'failover' to the backup system. We think this will open up the system to take new calls, but it will terminate current, ongoing calls. Do we have your permission to do so?"

Note that in doing so, we were already giving our stakeholders some degree of power over a situation that made them feel angry and powerless, by asking their OK to perform the failover.

Our customer's team talked briefly among themselves, asked me a couple questions then gave the OK. My engineer triggered the failover and nobody in the room breathed as we watched the system dashboard, waiting to see if calls would start going through again as the backup system came online. Fortunately it did and we all collectively sighed. Only for a moment. Then the shouting resumed.

They demanded to know why the system went down and what we were going to do to fix it. At that point, we had no idea what caused it, no idea how to fix it, and no idea if it was going to happen again in 5 minutes.

My response? "We don't know the root cause or if it will happen again. We are going to restart the primary system in case we need to fail-back again, and we are escalating to our product team and executive management. We don't expect to have a root cause in 30 minutes, but I will give you an update at that time, in this room."

This satisfied our customer enough to let us get to work. In 30 minutes we gave them an update on what we were doing, our next steps, and the fact that we didn't have a root cause identified yet. We met again every 30 minutes that day until we had a potential fix identified and a plan to implement it.

Every action item, every 30 minute update and every finding we had was documented in the Issue log. This way, our customer could reference it as they communicated to their stakeholders in the organization. This also gave our internal team - on-site and in the remote product support team - a common, accurate and up to date understanding of where we were, what we had done and what the next steps were.

48 very long and sleepless hours later, we had implemented one hotfix which failed spectacularly, had another emergency failover, and finally implemented a successful fix. Although those were 48 very difficult hours which we would have been happy to avoid, the fact that we actively managed the issue and communicated so well gave our customer confidence that we were going to resolve the issue. Looking back, it was clear that our successful management of this issue ended up building a stronger long-term relationship with the customer. And I still

feel that a key part of that was our use of an Issue Log to track and communicate that issue.

Issue Log FAQ

Question	Answer
Should I log every single little issue that comes up? Seems like a waste of time, especially if I already resolved it	If an issue impacted your schedule, your budget or any deliverables, or if it created subsequent risk to any aspect of the project, you should log it. You cannot learn from the issues you don't record.
Isn't an Issue log just a list of our failures? What's the point?	None of us likes to repeat the same mistakes over and over. So, every issue is an opportunity for learning. And if nothing else, you should be able to explain the problems that happened on the project to your sponsor

Additional Issue Management Resources

Podcast: *Project Management Happy Hour: Condition Red!* by Kim Essendrup and Kate Anderson, https://pmhappyhour.com/014-2

D = Decisions

Nobody knows everything about a project when it begins. All projects are exercises in progressive elaboration, learning more about the project, the deliverables and what you need to do to achieve them as you go along. In that journey, you will inevitably encounter decisions that have to be made; what color is the button? Where does the toilet get installed? Which of these conflicting stakeholders do we listen to? In every project, decisions have to be made and the Decision log gives you a way to plan, track and communicate those decisions.

> A Decision Log is not just a list of decisions; it is a method for driving effective decision making in your project

Case Study: Approval of the Workers

Many years ago I ran a project for a company based in Germany. They had employees all across Europe, and we were excited to partner with them to roll out a new technology which would affect the majority of those employees, making their work lives just a bit easier.

We planned the project well, execution was right on target, budget was on and all of our stakeholders were happy. Bringing in this expansive, complex project on-time and on-budget was going to be a major win.

Being a large, mature enterprise, this organization had very structured change control processes which had to be followed to implement change to the organization. This process culminated in a presentation to their Change Board. Having tripped-up on this process in a previous project, our team was ready this time, following every step, every process, and submitting all the required documentation. So, two weeks before our change was to be implemented, we went into the dreaded Change Board meeting confident that we were going to get a green light on our final go-live. If we didn't get approval in this meeting, we could be set back weeks or months.

In this meeting, made up of business and technology services executives, each project manager who had a pending change presented their proposed change, its risks and impacts, and asked for permission to proceed. When our turn came up, I presented our project, preemptively answering all the questions that I expected. I finished presenting and we were on the cusp of getting approval when one of the Change Board members said, almost off-handedly, "You have Workers Council approval on this, yes?"

(Gulp). "What is a Workers Council?"

As I would very quickly learn, the employees of large enterprises in some European countries, particularly Germany, may form a Workers Council. This council represents the company's employees to corporate leadership. Workers Councils can be incredibly powerful organizations, with the authority to stop or reverse decisions made by even the highest level of corporate management if the decision impacts employees. Since my project impacted employees, the Change Board was probably right to assume it required the approval of the Workers Council. Which I clearly did not have or even know about.

Better yet, the Workers Council for this organization only met once per quarter. So, instead of going live in two weeks, we were potentially facing a delay of months because I hadn't planned for Workers Council approval. How was I going to fund my team to hang around for a couple extra months waiting for approval? Did I just blow the timeline and budget for the entire project?

What is a Decision in a RAID Log?

The Decisions we track in a RAID log represent key "forks on the road" for our project. They include all the decisions that we can plan for through the lifecycle of our project (including Workers Council approval, in some cases), and ad-hoc decisions that can come up during the course of our projects.

Decisions can be about the project deliverables, about the activities required to produce the deliverables, or they can be about how your team works on a daily basis. Some typical examples include:

- **Scope Elaboration** – adding detail to the nature of the deliverables

- **Plan Elaboration** – adding detail to the process and activities needed to create the project's deliverables

- **Resources** – determining which resources and suppliers will be engaged

- **Risk Management** - deciding on response strategies and contingencies for project risk

- **Issue Management** - deciding how to handle issues when they come up

- **Stage Gates** - deciding whether or to proceed to the next stage of the project and, if so, if the project's plans should be changed.

Good decision making is not just about getting a decision made. As described in our case study, good decision making must involve all the appropriate stakeholders - whether that involvement is approval of the decision, or simply consultation and communication.

Why should I track Decisions?

Getting decisions wrong will cost you. Bad decision making can take your project down the wrong path, stop your project in its tracks, or cause delays and rework because necessary decisions were made incorrectly, by the wrong people, or not at all. Issues related to bad decision making generally fall into these categories:

- **Decisions don't get made.** Key decision points are not identified as needing broader stakeholder or customer input, so the team makes assumptions about how to proceed. In essence, this is making a decision - to not involve outside stakeholders. By the time the stakeholder or sponsor realizes the decision was made for them and that they don't like it, it's usually too late and significant rework is required and trust is lost with stakeholders.

- **Decisions are don't involve the right people.** Perhaps as bad as decisions not formally made are those that are made by the wrong stakeholders. This happens when not enough thought and communication are put into decision planning and the right decision makers are left out. This often leads to frustrated stakeholders, revisiting decisions, and rework.

- **Decisions don't get communicated to those impacted.** Key decisions can impact your team and stakeholders directly and indirectly. So, decisions and the process used to make them should be transparent to all those involved and affected. It's the PMs responsibility to communicate decisions to all those involved.

- **Decisions don't get implemented.** Even the best decision making is a waste of time if the outcome of the decision is not implemented. It's the PMs responsibility to track project decisions and act on them to ensure they are implemented.

- **Decisions don't get tracked and later cannot be explained.** Particularly in longer duration projects with many stakeholders, and those that are being implemented as part of a contractual agreement, decision making can be subject to high levels of scrutiny. Stakeholders may well revisit past decisions and demand justification for those decisions or push to change them. Without documentation, you may find yourself unable to explain how those decisions were made, why and by whom, leaving your project subject to the whim of stakeholders that want to remake past decisions.

What you don't want to happen is this: you get to the end of a project and your sponsor or customer says, "wait, who told you to do it this way? Who made the decision to this?" Your decision log should be thorough enough to back-up all the decisions made in the project so you can speak to it later, if needed.

A special case where you will wish you had strong decision documentation is when your sponsor or stakeholders change. Often these changes cannot be predicted, but what you can predict is that new stakeholders will want to have a say in how your project goes, which may include revisiting past decisions. You cannot necessarily prevent decisions from being remade in this circumstance, but you can make that process easier by explaining each decision made in the project, how it was made and why.

How do I use my Decision Log?

In its simplest form, a Decision log is just a list of the decisions that have to be made and those that have been made. But we want more than just a list; we want to drive effective decision making in our projects. To do that, here is a five step methodology we can use with our Decision log.

1. Identify Decisions that must be made

If you sit down with your team early in the project when doing your initial planning, you'll find that you can identify most of the important decisions and approvals that need to be made in your project in advance, giving you an opportunity to plan for them. As you identify them, they should all go into your Decision log.

You will also find that many decision points come up ad-hoc through the lifecycle of the project, and this is OK. It's just as important to get these decisions logged and managed through the same process as you do for decisions that you plan in advance.

Like our risk identification process, when we identify decisions, we want to capture not only the decision to be made, but the reason we need to have the decision made and its impacts. Like risks, this can be done in a problem / impact statement. For example:

- *We need to decide on a cloud hosting provider so we can start building out our infrastructure*

- *We need to decide whether or not to pass the planning gate to ensure our finalized plans still align with the approved budget and expected benefits or we could end up wasting resources and funds that could be spent on another project*

- *We need to approve the user acceptance testing results so we can ensure the system is working as expected before we roll it out to all our end users*

2. Identify who needs to make the decision

After identifying the decisions that need to be made, you need to identify the appropriate decision makers. If you've done a good job initiating your project and identifying the governance structure, the decision maker or makers should be clear for most decisions.

In cases where the decision maker is not so clear, you'll need to use your leadership, communication and stakeholder management skills to find the right person or group. You may find that you need to balance group-based consensus decision making with more directed decision making by a single person.

- Fewer (or sole) decision makers generally make decisions faster, more consistently and to a consistent vision. But more concentrated decision making risks not adequately engaging stakeholders.

- Consensus-based decision making benefits from broader stakeholder engagement which can increase long term support for your project, but they generally take longer and can sometimes result in less effective, less consistent decisions.

Sometimes you can balance this by identifying an executive decision maker, but soliciting feedback on the decision options and impacts from a broad group of stakeholders. This way your stakeholders have input into the decision and your executive decision maker can make a quicker decision with the confidence they have support of the stakeholders.

3. Identify the Options of the Decision

Where you can, identify the options available for each decision and the follow-on impacts of each. Include the positives, the negatives and the unknowns for each decision option, like in a T-chart, below. You'll likely need to engage your team, your stakeholders and maybe even outside advisors to understand the available options and their impacts. The effort is worth it, though; a sound understanding of the options available not only helps you more effectively communicate the decision to your decision makers, but also helps them make better and more informed decisions.

One of the most important options to include may be that of no decision, or to do nothing. Most decisions have a date by which they must be made to avoid impacts to the project. To help prioritize decisions and communicate their urgency, document the impacts if the decision is not made by the required date.

> *Example: If we do not select all our speakers for the event by July 1, then we won't be able to include their photos and bio in the conference mailer, reducing the number of registrations from people who would have been interested to see those unlisted speakers*

Once you have an understanding of the impacts of a decision, reevaluate the decision makers, ensuring that they are still appropriate considering the options and impacts.

The Paradox of Choice

In his book The Paradox of Choice, Barry Schwartz discusses how people like to have choices; but too many choices can lead to decision paralysis. By identifying decision options we create an informed, limited list of choices for our decision makers. They can of course choose a different option, but asking "which of these options do you want to choose?" will nearly always lead to better decision making than presenting infinite choices by asking, "what do you want to do?"

---

4. Get the Decision Made

Don't take for granted that you know how the decision will be made, even if you know the decision makers and have researched the options for the decision. Start by simply asking your decision maker(s) how they will make the decision, and what information they think they will need to make a sound decision.

Regardless of who they are, it is always advisable to communicate with the decision maker well in advance of when the decision is needed, providing the facts, options, impacts and deadline for the decision. It is also a good idea to have a recommendation ready to help advise the decision makers. As the project leader, your advice matters, so be ready with a recommendation for what you think is the best option.

5. Act on the Decision

The best made decisions in the world are worthless if they are not acted on. When the decision is made, immediately document that decision in your RAID log and list the actions that need to be performed in order to implement it, adding assignments and due dates. This process makes for a good discussion with the decision makers at the time the decision is made.

One of the most important actions is communicating the decision to impacted stakeholders and team members. This can of course be done by sharing this part of your RAID log, but often decisions will require additional communication and alignment. Be sure that is accounted for in your decision actions.

Tips on executive decision making

When working with executives to get a decision made, be careful to present the right level of detail. If you drill down too deep, your executives might get lost in the details and miss the big picture. Highlight the impact to the project's goals and its stakeholders first so they understand the big picture, then take them through additional layers of detail if needed.

It is good practice to have backup detail at the ready if needed, in case your executives start asking hard questions and drilling down. If you are presenting using a PowerPoint, for example, have a hidden section at the end with "backup slides" of detailed data that you can refer to if needed.

Tips on facilitating group decisions

If you have to get group consensus for a decision, a good strategy is to engage individually with each decision maker first, before presenting to the group as a whole for the decision. Start with the most opinionated or influential stakeholders first, then gradually work your way out to other stakeholders, building consensus individually, then in pairs or smaller groups behind the scenes. With this strategy, you will go into the final decision making meeting with the support and buy-in of the individuals involved, making for a more efficient and predictable group decision. If you can at all avoid it, never walk into a group decision making meeting 'cold' and try to get a decision made.

Document the decision in front of decision making groups

Whatever the process you use and however many decision makers are involved, when the decision is made you should document the decision in front of them in your Decision log. This is a great way to codify decisions. One of my colleagues used this to great effect; as she worked with her executive stakeholders to get a decision made, she would share her Decision log via Zoom or overhead projector, typing the exact decision and listing the names of everyone in the room as decision makers. You can bet that when the executives saw their name going down next to a decision, they paid quite a lot more attention to the decision being made!

What if I can't get a critical decision made? Or I'm forced to revisit a past decision?

For decisions that you are having trouble getting made, you may need to escalate to your sponsor for support and direction. Hopefully with their help, you can get the decision made.

If a decision doesn't get made by the required date or if you are forced to revisit and remake a past decision, these become issues so should go into your Issue log and get handled as such. For decisions that are being revisited and changed, be sure to let the decision makers know what the impacts are of re-making the decision. If they insist on proceeding, track this as another decision (rather than changing the previous decision entry in your log). If this impacts your project, track it also as a related Issue. And if the decision results in a need for additional funds, resources, time or a change in scope, it may also make sense to include a project change request as part of remaking the decision.

Case Study Conclusion: Decision of the Workers

Back in my Change Board meeting, I was still standing there, wondering what a Workers Council was. Fortunately I had my project sponsor sitting-in with me for support. He fully understood what was at stake when I was asked about Workers Council approval, and immediately jumped in.

"We shouldn't need Workers Council approval on this, but I will socialize it with them to be sure. Can we get your conditional approval on this project change, assuming we can get confirmation from the Workers Council that they are OK with it?"

The Change Board agreed, giving us the OK to proceed with the change on the condition that we received approval from the Workers Council - or confirmation that they didn't care. Immediately after the meeting, my sponsor went to work, reaching out to key members of the Workers Council to socialize our project and get their support. He must have done a great job, because he managed to get the Workers Council to hold an emergency meeting specifically to approve our project. Several days later, we went live as scheduled, and I had a whole new level of appreciation for people who can get decisions made in large European enterprises.

Decision Log FAQ

Question	Answer
What if I cannot get an important decision made?	If you are having problems getting a decision made, then raise it as a Risk and, if appropriate, raise it to your project sponsor for support. If it doesn't get made by the Decision Date, it is probably now an Issue and should be documented and escalated as such.
Why should I go through the work of identifying options? It's my decision maker's responsibility to make the decision, not mine.	That's true, but as a project manager, it is very much in your interest to ensure decisions are made well the first time. So, taking the time to help your decision makers understand the options and what's at stake helps them make better decisions. Otherwise, you risk poor decision making and revisiting past decisions - both of which are much more costly than investing time in researching the decision

Additional Decision Management Resources

- Podcast: *Project Management Happy Hour: Stage Direction in the Board Room* by Kim Essendrup and Kate Anderson, https://pmhappyhour.com/ep019

- Book: *Getting to Yes* by Fisher, Ury and Patton. Penguin Publishing Group, 2011.

- Book: *Crucial Conversations* by Patterson, Grenny, Mcmillan and Switzler. McGraw Hill, 2021

- Book: *The Paradox of Choice* by Barry Schwartz. Ecco, 2017.

Wait, I Thought A=Assumptions and D=Dependencies?

Question: I thought the "A" and "D" in RAID stood for Assumptions and Dependencies?!

If you have used a RAID log before, you may have heard that the "A" and "D" in RAID stand for Assumptions and Dependencies. But in this book, we use Actions and Decisions instead - a seemingly small difference that has a huge impact on how your RAID log is used.

An Assumption is a condition that is assumed to be true when the scope, schedule and budget of your project were put together. For example, your project may be planned with the assumption that you have qualified developers in your organization, or that a system you are replacing will be operational until a certain date. Ideally these planning assumptions are documented at the same time the plan is.

A Dependency is something delivered by a party external to your project team, upon which some or all of your project depends on. For example, you may have an external dependency on the utility company turning-up power to your project site before the HVAC contractors can test the heating and cooling systems. You and your HVAC contractors need the power company to perform this activity, but since the power company is not on your project team, you may have little authority over this external dependency.

Assumptions and Dependencies are clearly important and should be tracked. They both carry an inherent risk in that if they do not happen as expected, your project will be impacted. For this reason, they should be treated as Risks in your RAID log, right alongside all your other risks. They are subject to the same analysis, prioritization, response planning and communication as any other risk. In fact, collecting all the assumptions and dependencies is the best way to start off your Risk log. This is why, <u>with one notable exception which we will cover later</u>, we typically treat Assumptions and Dependencies as Risks, not as separate categories of items.

Some project managers I work with prefer not to put dependencies in their RAID log, but feel they should be managed from their project schedule. This is quite useful as well as dependencies often have schedule impacts.

The most important difference between tracking Assumptions & Dependencies vs Actions & Decisions in a RAID log is how and when they are managed - which is why we treat them the way we do.

- Assumptions & Dependencies are typically identified at the beginning of a project and are input into the schedule and risk planning early on, then monitored through the project.

- Action items & Decisions for the most part, have to be actively managed throughout the entire lifecycle of the project and must constantly be captured and tracked.

PART 3: HOW DO I RUN MY PROJECT WITH MY RAID LOG?

A RAID log is more than a spreadsheet. It's a method for running your project, keeping you focused on what you need to do today, this week and next week to keep your project on track.

Remember that projects usually don't go wrong because of the tasks themselves. They go wrong because of unmanaged risks, out of control issues, forgotten action items and poor decisions.

> Projects don't go wrong because of the tasks themselves. They go bad because of unmanaged risks, out of control issues, forgotten action items and poor decisions.

Managing you RAID Log

So far we've covered each individual tab of a RAID log and how to manage each one. But now let's discuss how to effectively use your RAID log as a whole to manage your project.

Who owns the RAID log?

The RAID log should be owned and maintained by the person responsible for getting the initiative done. For a project, this would be the Project Manager. For teams that work more agile, it could be the Product Owner or SCRUM master. It could be a team leader, or a change manager in charge of an organizational transformation. In any case, the person who is hands-on and responsible for the day-to-day management and execution of the initiative should be the owner of the RAID log.

RAID Review Approach

Contrary to the spelling, when you review your RAID, it is usually best to follow the sequence I-R-D-A.

1. **Issues** - review your open issues in priority order, ensuring your remediation plans are up to date and that impacted stakeholders are up to date and

communicated with. When you have critical open issues, you may not get further in your RAID log until the issue is resolved.

2. **Risks** - Sort by risk score (P*I) and by trigger date if you are using that field. Check up on your remediation activities to make sure they are on track and then think through any additional risks that may have come up since your last review.

3. **Decisions** - filter for open decisions and sort by the decision date. Review each to ensure you are on track with plans to get the decision made. Identify any open decisions where you still haven't figured out the options or the decision makers and work on those.

4. **Action Items** - filtering for open items that have impending due dates.

   - If something can be done in 2 minutes or less, do it now. This is part of David Allen's Getting Things done methodology. If you don't, you'll end up spending more time managing the action item than it would take for you to get it done.

   - Ensure all items have a due date and assignee. If some are missing, work on that.

   - Review items assigned to you - and wherever possible, delegate!

   - Prioritize those Action Items that are important and have a long term effect on the project over those that are urgent and less important.

Ideal times to perform this review are with your regularly scheduled team meetings, or when preparing your regular status reports - which may be at the same time. We'll talk more about timing for RAID reviews (daily, weekly, etc.) in the next section of this book.

Where do I put my RAID log?

There are several options for building and sharing your RAID log: spreadsheet files, online spreadsheet sharing hosts like Google Sheets or Microsoft online, or one of a handful of online applications which let you effectively manage a RAID log, like RAIDLOG.com. But don't get hung up on which application you use. Jump in and start doing it!

When evaluating options, you may get tempted to break up your RAID log and use different apps – maybe an online task management app for Action Items, and maybe you have different apps or documents where you could manage Risks, Issues or Decisions. You need to find what works best for you and your team, but generally, you will have better results if you can keep core RAID items (Risks, Issues, Actions and Decisions) in one place where you can manage them together. Task switching inherently disrupts the flow of work and forces you to lose out on the simplicity and efficiency that makes a RAID log so effective.

> ## Tip:
> Switching between apps disrupts the flow of work and reduces efficiency, so it's best to keep all your RAID log items together in one place

Spreadsheets

The most common hosting method for a RAID log is a simple spreadsheet file. Most everyone who can use a computer can use a spreadsheet, so a Microsoft Excel file has long been the default format for RAID logs. The challenge with a file based solution is making your RAID accessible to others. For this reason, a file based RAID is usually best for small projects or highly secure or dynamic projects where you need tight control over your RAID. This approach also works when you are just starting out and haven't had time yet to figure out a long term hosting solution.

Online: Google Sheets, Microsoft Online

One of the best options for hosting your RAID log is an online file sharing service like Google Sheets, Microsoft Online or other spreadsheet hosting software. This is much more efficient than using a spreadsheet file on your computer because these services store data online where it is always up to date and always accessible. You can also manage permissions to some extent, allowing some team members to edit your RAID and others to only view it. Plus, these services can sometimes track versions, giving you the ability to roll back changes if needed.

Purpose-b0075ilt Project Management Tools

There are also purpose-built applications for managing projects. These tools can be pretty advanced, giving you an online tool to manage your project schedules, empowering teams with automation, fine-grained access management, reporting and analytics. Unfortunately, many of these tools do a mediocre job of RAID management, and they usually require a significant investment.

When it comes to selecting a platform for hosting your RAID log, keep in mind this advice:

- Keep it simple. You should spend more time using your RAID log than trying to make your RAID log tooling work

- Keep it accessible. You should be able to share the document to whom you want, and control who can access it.

- Keep it secure. Your organization probably has information security policies regarding project data. Ensure that you understand those policies and follow them.

If you are ready to move past a simple spreadsheet but haven't decided on another solution, check out RAIDLOG.com for an alternative.

PART 4: HOW DO I USE MY RAID TO

Now that we've described what a RAID log is and how to host it, let's talk about how this simple tool can take you and your project to the next level.

Be an ultimate PM, always on top of everything

Project management can be totally overwhelming. Meetings, problems, people, deadlines and oh, so many emails. With all that going on, it is easy to get overwhelmed with all the things you need to do and start falling behind. This is where your RAID log becomes more than a document - it becomes a methodology.

The goal of your RAID log is to help you keep operationally aware and on top of your projects. It is more than a document - it is your PM superpower.

Reviewing your RAID log should be your quiet moment where you get your head together and plan your day or week. The key is planning ahead and giving yourself time to review your RAID log. If you don't plan it in advance and time-box a part of your work week to it, RAID review is the kind of thing that gets put aside and becomes another thing you fall behind on.

Weekly Review

At the minimum, block some time on Friday morning, first thing before you open your email to review and update your RAID once per week. This will give you an opportunity to make your updates from the week's accomplishments, plan for the next week and get your updates in line for your weekly status report if you do that kind of thing.

> Your RAID should be your "good morning" application. Block off quiet time to focus on your RAID items before opening your mailbox to the chaos of the day

Daily Check-in

If you are going to go all in with your RAID log, then go with a daily review - especially if you have a heavy project load or projects on fire. First thing in the morning, before you open Outlook and while your first cup of coffee is still hot, open your RAID log (or logs if you manage multiple projects), and do a quick run-through. Identify 'must do' items for the day and either block time for them on your calendar, or write them on your to-do list or post-it notes.

Replace my meeting notes, now and forever

One of the best PM's I know, the one who introduced me to RAID logs, lived by them daily. Her projects of choice were merger & acquisition projects, where she worked with the leadership of acquired and acquiring organizations to plan and implement the merge of business functions. This is really challenging work – the executives she worked with knew that not everyone at the table would have a seat at the end of the process. This meant that meetings were high stakes and there was often little incentive to cooperate.

When I asked her how she facilitated these contentious meetings and got anything done, she said "I don't use meeting notes. I use my RAID log!" She took no meeting notes at all! The logic is simple:

- When you plan and facilitate a meeting, what are the most important things you need to do in that meeting? Identify and discuss Risks and Issues, make Decisions, and track the Action items that follow.

- What are the most important outputs of meetings, the things that must be captured in meeting minutes and acted on after the fact? **Risks, Actions, Issues and Decisions.**

What's left that's worth capturing in your notes? Not much.

Maybe the best part of this approach is that you don't have to spend 30-60 minutes of your life after every meeting drafting minutes - or feeling guilty that you didn't. You've already captured the most important part of the meeting in real-time.

I challenge you to try it! Try to run one of your regular status, governance or planning meetings using your RAID log as much as possible. Whenever there is a new Action, Issue, or Decision, share your RAID log and type it out real-time, and see how much more everyone pays attention. And see how much time you save by not having to do minutes afterward.

A quick tip here - if you are going to try to replace your meeting notes with your RAID, make it easy to find which items in your RAID log came from which meeting. Add a column in your RAID log for "Source" or "Meeting" and add the meeting name and date. That lets you quickly find all the items pertinent to a particular meeting.

Rescue a failing project

Many project managers get to a point in their career where they are so trusted at achieving results that they are called in as "Cleaners" to sort things out when a project goes wrong. Think of Winston Wolf from Pulp Fiction, but with a PMP instead of a bow tie.

Having had this role myself and having seen many of my colleagues do the same, I can say from experience that there is absolutely no better tool to get a problem project under control than a RAID log. Nothing. I can also say that I have never had to rescue a project that had an up to date RAID log.

The RAID log story I share in the introduction and conclusion of this book is a perfect example how to use a RAID log to get a problem project under control. Here's a brief summary of the process I use.

1. *Show me your RAID log.* Once you land and get an understanding of who the stakeholders are and what the situation is, one of your first tactical questions should be, "Can you show me your RAID log?" First, it establishes that you know what you are doing. If the project is that bad off, odds are they don't have one or even know what a RAID log is. Secondly, it puts responsibility back on the team – if they had a RAID log and had been managing to it, they wouldn't need you right now.

2. You will almost always find that there is no existing RAID log. If there is, it probably hasn't been touched in months and is worthless, so don't use it. Start a new log from scratch and don't transfer anything over from the old one.

TIP:
Use the process of building your RAID log as a structured way to perform discovery and engage the team and stakeholders in the discussion

---

3. Start with Issues, as identified by your stakeholders. The most important thing when getting your hands around a broken project is understanding all the current issues and their impacts. Take time to listen to each of the key stakeholders and understand each issue. Focus on being a good listener and

let your stakeholders express all their frustrations. Drill down into the specific impacts of each issue, being careful to understand what feedback is driven by emotion and what is driven by the real impacts of the issue. We're not in problem solving mode right now – you just need to capture all the issues and understand them before you can prioritize and act on them.

4. Now, review the issues as your team sees them. Like with the stakeholders, give them a chance to talk through their frustrations, and be careful to separate fact from emotion, while giving them room to be angry or frustrated. They are probably pretty beat-up by the time the "Cleaner" got called in.

5. Now, Risks. Things have gone wrong and you may be in the middle of a crisis. But however bad things are, they can always get worse. Get clarity on the things that can still go wrong and make the current situation worse, and get them into your Risk log.

6. At this point, it's time for some tough conversations around Decisions. The first decision in the project was to do the project, which was made with assumptions about how the project would be executed. If our project is in major trouble, you should have the sponsor revisit that initial decision and confirm if the project is still worth saving, or if they should make a decision to end the project. Ending a troubled project is never an easy decision, but it is the right decision much more often than it actually happens.

7. Action Items. Throughout this process, you have undoubtedly had a lot of action items come up which you've tracked in your RAID log. But now, to rescue this project, you need to transcend mere to-do items. You will need to lay out an action plan, a "Go to Green" plan. Tactically, this can be part of your Action Item log or it may even warrant another new tab specifically to manage your "Go to Green" plan.

Now, stay on top of all those items on a daily basis and your communication, and you will have the best possible chance of the best resolution.

Mercy killing

Sometimes, the best resolution is to not save a troubled project, but to kill it off. Killing a project that is doomed to fail is not a failure. Letting a doomed project continue to burn resources and cash is the real failure. Terminating a doomed project early enough can save millions in investment, uncounted hours of resource time, and free up the organization to focus on initiatives that can succeed. But even in this circumstance, don't forget your RAID log. You will want to plan, manage, and document the decision to terminate the project in your Decision log, just as you would any other critical decision.

No Project Tools? No problem.

I've built a consulting business around implementing project and portfolio management tools, so I get the opportunity to work with a lot of organizations across many fields. And it constantly surprises me how many organizations don't have the most basic tools to offer their project managers, the very people they are entrusting their organization's multi-million dollar capital budgets and critical changes with.

A recent trend is to implement one of the light task management solutions on the market (Asana, Trello, Jira, etc.) and call it a "project management" solution. The problem with this approach is that "doing tasks" is not where projects go wrong. So, task management apps aren't going to help avoid project problems. RAID logs, on the other hand, are purpose built to help project managers succeed.

> "Doing tasks" is not where projects go wrong. So, Task management apps aren't going to help you avoid project problems.

Even when organizations invest in more sophisticated Project and Portfolio Management (PPM) tools, very often they only license them for project managers so they can save on cost. This is an incredible waste because project information needs to be available to a large and often-times distributed set of stakeholders – most especially the project team. What good is a carefully curated project plan and project data repository if nobody but the Project Manager is licensed to see it? With a RAID log, you have the ability to collaborate with internal and external team members, stakeholders and clients.

In some specific cases, tool selection is limited due to organizational differences. Take the case of M&A (merger & acquisition) projects. Because they involve combining two different organizations, there is no common toolset across both organizations. Even if there are existing tools, they belong to one 'side' or the other. So, worst case, not everyone can access the tools, and best case, you look like you are choosing sides if you pick one over the other. In this case, a RAID log is a neutral tool you can use to run your project.

My perspective is that, as the Project Manager, you are the CEO of your project. So, whether you have no tool, the wrong tool, or tools that don't quite get the job done, you should feel empowered to use whatever tools you need to get the job done. And one of the easiest tools for you to acquire and use? A RAID log of course!

Managing Up - Project Reviews with my Manager and Sponsors

One aspect of project management that takes time and experience to develop is the ability to "manage up." This involves communicating with your sponsors and management stakeholders and engaging them in active support for your project. When you sit with your management team – direct managers or project sponsors – you need to do a couple things:

1. Make very efficient use of the limited time that you have with them

2. Be prepared to answer questions and concerns they may have

3. Put them to work

RAID is perfect for this. Your management team won't be interested in your tactical actions (unless their name is on them), but they should be interested in open issues, decisions and critical risks. In particular, focus on decisions; the ones they need to make or the decisions they need to help get made by others. Sponsors with something at stake in your project want to feel like they are involved and helping to move the project ahead. If you don't give them something constructive to do, they may try to add their own version of "help" and get uncomfortably involved in your project.

Manage Down - Project Reviews for my PM's

If you manage project managers or if you are a project sponsor and want to be actively engaged in your project's activities, a regularly scheduled RAID log review is a great way to monitor and support PM's and their projects in a structured way without micromanaging. These reviews both set expectations and provide a coaching opportunity.

To do this, schedule a recurring 1:1 meeting with your PM on a weekly, bi-weekly or monthly basis, depending on the scale and risk level of the project. The agenda will simply be a review of the RAID log. You can either keep this review high level by focusing only on the highest priority items, or you can drill down into the details, depending on how granular you want to get.

As the project manager presents their RAID log, check in and give feedback on their approach, level of detail and how they are managing RAID items through to completion. It's the perfect tool for a positive comprehensive review and for providing constructive feedback.

Ensure I CYA

One of the worst feelings in the world is working late into the night, combing through emails and project artifacts in a panicked rush to document and justify your team's past actions. This often happens when a project goes off track and you have to explain it to your management team or stakeholders.

Although the term CYA (cover your ass) definitely fits here, I'm not a fan of that term or the underlying philosophy. We want to be proactive and solve problems, not focus on keeping ourselves and our team from getting into trouble. But the reality is that things are going to go wrong at some point on some of your projects. When it does, you will be questioned about what went wrong, and you will have to explain what you and your team did about it.

If you have an up-to-date RAID log, you are covered - it is a detailed historical log of your project. Every issue should have been recorded. Every date slip, every decision made and every response you had to potential risks. The level of detail you track in your log is up to you and the conditions you and your team are working in. But it's better to spend a few extra minutes a week keeping your RAID log up to date than having to spend hours late at night combing through past emails, calendars and your memory trying to reconstruct historical events and justify your team's actions. If you've been a PM long enough, you know exactly what I mean.

When there are contracts involved or government agencies, the stakes are exponentially higher for project issues, so you should be taking your RAID log very seriously. If your project goes really wrong and there is any litigation around non-performance, your RAID log (or lack thereof) could end up a focal point of the proceedings. The advice I give project managers is this: Treat your RAID log like it is subject to subpoena - because one day, it may be.

> Treat your RAID log like it is subject to subpoena - because one day, it may be

Status Reporting

Regular status reporting is the cornerstone of good project communication. Status reporting not only keeps your sponsor and stakeholders up to date, bringing key items to their attention, but it is also a regular self-accountability check-in to help ensure you stay up to date on your projects.

Status reports should include progress information (plan vs actual) for schedule, scope delivery and budget, but they should also include key items from your RAID log including open issues, impending and new risks, and upcoming and recently made decisions. If you are tracking supplemental data in your RAID, which we cover later on, a change log and milestone tracker are also important status items.

If your RAID log is up to date, it's easy to simply copy & paste this information from your RAID log right into your status communications. I have a few long-time colleagues who manage teams of project managers and say RAID log data is the most important part of a status report.

Manage a Portfolio or Program

A program is a project made up of sub-projects or workstreams, all working together to achieve a broader goal. Each sub-project is often run by a different project manager. Being a program manager can be tough because not only do you have responsibility over the program as a whole, but you also have to manage multiple project managers, each of which may have their own way of doing things.

An easy way to help your PMs to manage things consistently and for you to help manage how they deliver is to have them all use RAID logs - ideally the same template. Then you can schedule a regular RAID log review meeting to coach your PMs and keep things coordinated across workstreams.

Not only can your RAID review be a way to provide oversight on workstream delivery, but you can aggregate the top issues, risks and decisions from individual workstreams into your program level RAID log. This won't be all you need of course, because there are always program level items which are not specific to any single workstream. So, you should be running your own Program level RAID as well.

For Programs specifically, it can be very useful to have a separate Dependencies log for tracking inter-workstream dependencies. These dependencies are an important topic for frequent reviews with your workstream leads and will help avoid a lot of miscommunication and planning issues.

> For Programs specifically, it can be very useful to have a separate Dependencies log for tracking inter-workstream dependencies.

Keep my customer on task by "Dependency Surfing"

Ever feel like you are always behind on your projects and that your customer or stakeholders are getting frustrated, always waiting on you? Try dependency surfing!

Dependency surfing works like this: If the customer constantly feels like they are waiting on you, they perceive you as the cause of project delays, holding things up even if you are on schedule and delivering as committed. But if you keep your customer or stakeholders busy with work that moves the project ahead, then they feel like you are on top of things and driving value, and they will have a vested interest in the project because of their involvement. It also helps keep them out of trouble ;-)

I call it dependency surfing because it often feels in a project like there is a relentless, rolling wave of things that need to be done - decisions, actions, issues to be managed. And if you are just a little bit behind, it can feel like that giant wave of things that needs to get done is continually crashing down on your head, leaving you gasping for air.

But, if you can get just that little bit ahead of that wave of activities and ride the crest - you can steer it, moving it forward instead of being mashed down into the sea bottom. Do this by staying on top of action items, finding ways to delegate and assign work - especially those that seem to be 'on your back,' so you can spend your time managing the delivery of activities rather than performing them. Strive to have more action items out there that people, especially your stakeholders, owe you than you owe in return.

If you try this, you will find that your customers and stakeholders actually love this. They feel the push to move things ahead, and tend to be satisfied that you are driving the project ahead. They are also pleased to be able to contribute to the project and their own success.

PART 5: What else can I put in my RAID log?

Risks, Actions, Issues and Decisions are the fundamental building blocks of a RAID log which keep you operationally present and on top of your project. But there are a lot of other useful things you can put into your RAID log that can be helpful on a daily basis.

That said, we do have to be careful not to go too crazy. Adding too many things to a RAID log distracts from the key things we need to focus on. The litmus test for whether something should go into your RAID log or not is this:

- Is it something that changes on a frequent basis - at least weekly?

- Is it something I have to remind people of on a weekly basis?

- Is it something I need repeated, quick access to?

- Is it something I need to use to keep my plan (schedule, resources and budget) on track?

If so, then it may be a good candidate for your RAID log. Otherwise, it could be baggage that could drag down the RAID, so may be better stored elsewhere.

Following are a few common RAID log additions. At one time or another I've used every one of these. You may add one or more of these to your RAID log - or come up with your own.

For each of the following additional RAID log tabs, we have included a list of recommended columns for your RAID log in the appendix.

L = Lessons Learned

The best time to capture lessons learned is as you learn them! So why not use a tool to do so that is always handy during your project – your RAID log. Long term, this may be one of the most valuable ways to extend your RAID log.

Capturing lessons learned allows you to take a positive, constructive action following both problems and pleasant surprises that may come up. For example, in your meeting where you resolve an issue or remediate a risk, you can immediately flip over to your Lessons Learned log and prompt the team, "OK, now what are the lessons we need to take away from this experience for next time?"

All resolved Issues should find their way into your Lessons Learned log. There is a school of thought that your Issue log should be your Lessons Learned log. The problem with this approach is that you can learn as much or more from things that went right as you can from things that went wrong. But logging things that went really well in your Issues log to capture positive lessons learned is more than a little awkward.

All that said, simply documenting a lesson learned in a log somewhere doesn't actually help anyone. You need to turn each lesson into action, whether it be changing a process, updating documents or incorporating the lesson into future planning. To do this, lessons learned should be revisited at the end of each iteration, phase or at the end of the project, so you can make an action plan to respond to each lesson learned.

D = Dependencies

Earlier in this book I discussed why I prefer to use Actions and Decisions over Assumptions and Dependencies as the "A" and "D" in my RAID log. But as I will share in a case study at the end of this book, tracking dependencies in a RAID log can be one of the best ways to turn a troubled project around. And as mentioned earlier, tracking inter-workstream dependencies is a critical part of program management.

Dependency tracking can also be useful when managing a difficult customer or partner organization. For example, if you are delivering for a customer that seems to have a hard time meeting their obligations, it can be very useful to have a Dependency log to track those obligations and hold the customer accountable.

This is particularly powerful if those dependencies are contracted obligations on the part of the customer or partner.

If you are tracking dependencies, they should always be deliverable focused. This means that these are possibly (maybe even likely) redundant to your project plan. But it is sometimes worth it to be able to quickly pull up all the dependencies for an organization and hold them accountable.

C = Change Log

"What changed? When and why?" These are questions that, as a PM, you need to be able to answer at any time on a project. If you're not aware of all the changes on your project, then who is?

Tracking change is a fundamental skill and responsibility of a project manager. Any time there is a change to any parameter, the PM must identify the change, evaluate the impact and raise it to the sponsors for evaluation. Although schedule, scope and cost are the most common parameters to track, changes to resources, stakeholders and sponsors are just as important.

This is where your RAID log can shine. RAID log is a great place to maintain a centralized list of all changes in the project, whether they are approved or not, still being researched or newly identified.

Rather than a dedicated Change log on your RAID, many PMs prefer to track project changes in the Decision log. I sometimes prefer this approach, myself, with a column denoting the nature of the change so I can easily filter out decisions specific to project changes. Whether you track change requests as a decision or a separate log is a judgment call you will need to make. As long as they are logged one way or another, you'll be fine.

C = Contact List / Stakeholder Register

For projects with large teams or many stakeholders, it can be very useful to incorporate a contact list into your RAID log. This is particularly useful at the beginning of a project when you are still getting to know everyone. Completing and sharing a contact list can also be a nice way to clarify everyone's role on the project and to communicate those roles to everyone involved.

Quick tip: include the stakeholder's timezone if you have stakeholders and team members in different parts of the country or world.

R = RACI Matrix

You can develop your list of contacts further by expanding it into a RACI matrix. If you aren't familiar with this tool, it documents the roles and responsibilities for everyone involved in your project. It works by creating a matrix of each team member and stakeholder on one axis, and all the key activities and responsibilities on another. For each responsibility, you map out which stakeholders are Accountable for the success of the activity, Responsible for hands-on performance, Consulted about how the work should be done or Informed about progress.

This can be very useful to keep on hand when there are a lot of stakeholders and team members and where the PM may need to actively keep resources aligned to their responsibilities. It's nice to be able to say:

> *"Actually, that is/is not your responsibility. Here, let me pull up our agreed RACI matrix for that job..."*

You can list roles, responsibilities and even who should receive different communications like status reports in the RACI matrix.

R = Resource Calendar / Resource Plan

On the topic of resources, you can also create a Resource Calendar or a Resource Plan in your RACI matrix. Although, if you have a scheduling tool, that may be a better place to keep that information. Even so, it can be very handy to key resource dates like travel dates, vacation days, etc. in your RAID log. If you have an international project, this is a great place to track international holidays which can easily sneak up on you and impact your schedule.

Resource calendars and even entire resource plans can be managed in a RAID log if there is no other good place for the PM to keep this information. These can be in a calendar format, identifying personal vacations and observed holidays, or a more detailed resource plan like the illustration below.

M = Milestones / Deliverables and signoffs

If you are delivering a project to a customer or if your organization is really focused on deliverable acceptance, then a useful extension for your RAID log is a simple table to track milestone deliverables, their due dates and status.

Personally, I've used this to great effect on services engagements where we had to frequently track and report on our progress for scoped deliverables which rolled up into payment milestones. It was very handy to have that list on the RAID log, easy to access with my client and with my own management team who was very interested in progress toward payment milestones. This also made status reporting easy, as I could simply copy and paste that table into my status report

S = Project Schedule

I've seen many PM's track their entire project schedule in their RAID log. We talk about this in the Action Item section of this book, and why this shouldn't be your first choice. There are better tools for developing and managing complex project schedules. But honestly, for a basic project schedule, a tab in your RAID log will get it done.

The challenge is there is a temptation to basically rebuild a project scheduling tool like Microsoft Project out of Excel - a trap myself and many other project managers have fallen into. If you do need to build your schedule in a RAID log, I'd recommend keeping it simple. And even if you do put your Schedule in your RAID Log, I still recommend keeping your Project Schedule and Action Items separate. I discuss the reasons why they should be separate and how to decide if something belongs in Action Items or as part of your Project schedule in the Action Items section earlier in this book.

PART 6: But we're Agile! Why would I need a RAID?

Agile ways of working have significantly impacted project delivery for the better. Prioritizing people over processes, focusing on deliverables over documentation, being open to collaboration and responding to change all improve the efficiency of delivery. But does that mean there are no more risks? Does that mean issues are a thing of the past and that action items and decisions are no longer relevant? Of course not. A RAID log is just as useful and relevant whether you follow an agile methodology or a more predictive "waterfall" methodology.

And let's be real. While agile thinking espouses communication over documentation, if you're in an area of responsibility, something goes wrong, and an exec says, "what happened here? Why didn't this go as expected? What did you do about it?" You and your team need to have an answer - an answer you can get from your RAID log.

Product & Team Oriented RAID

If your organization is following a more agile-centric methodology and there is no formal project management role, then who would manage a RAID log? In these cases, it's typically the Product Owner and the SCRUM Master.

For the Product Owner, they can use RAID to manage their product, tracking risks, actions, issues and decisions needed to make the product succeed. For the SCRUM master or team lead, RAID tends to be more tactical, focusing on the things that help the agile team succeed, fueling those all-important retrospectives.

Agile Risk

One reason that agile ways of working have become so popular is that they inherently reduce risk by planning for change, tightening collaboration and delivering work in smaller bites. This approach definitely reduces overall risk. But working in an agile way does not eliminate risk and issues. Things still can and do go wrong. So, how do agile ways of working suggest addressing this?

The body of knowledge around Agile Risk management is still a bit thin. Some agile frameworks like DSDM acknowledge risk without providing much detail on how to manage it, while other frameworks cover risk in passing, if at all. This is an evolving area of practice and will certainly develop over the coming years.

In one of the few books on the topic, "Agile Risk Management" by Dr. Alan Moran, the author recommends an approach that is exactly in-line with traditional project risk management. This includes analyzing organizational tolerance for risk and developing a "Risk List." Like more traditional project management, Dr. Moran recommends that your risk management approach be scaled to the level of risk in the project and the risk tolerance of the organization.

If the body of knowledge around agile risk management is thin, it's even thinner for critical issue management, decision making and managing action items. So, if you work in an agile way, give a RAID log a chance - you may find it as useful as any other delivery leader.

PART 7: RAID FAQ

I have coached hundreds of project managers in the effective use of RAID logs, and helped many organizations successfully adopt them. Following are some of the most common questions that come up when starting to use RAID logs.

What if none of the other PMs in my org use a RAID Log?

If you are the first, you probably won't be the last. Once someone takes the initiative to start using a RAID log in an organization, it usually spreads like wildfire. Even if it doesn't, you'll have a great tool which gives you an edge in managing your own projects. So, if you're the first in your org to use a RAID log, don't let that hold you back. Be the thought leader!

What if nobody's looking at my RAID?

You can put a lot of work into your RAID log only to find that you are the only person who cares. Honestly, that is perfectly OK if your RAID log is helping you deliver more effectively. Even so, RAID logs are a great opportunity to collaborate with your team and stakeholders. To get the most out of the collaboration potential, check yourself on the following:

- Are you keeping your RAID up to date? Nobody is interested in looking at stale data.

- Do you use your RAID in your status reports and communications?

- Do you communicate to your team that your RAID log is the source of truth? For anyone else to treat it with importance, they must perceive that you also view it as important.

Make sure your up-to-date RAID log is incorporated into your regular project team discussions and communications. And really, even if none of your stakeholders are opening the document, you have a tool you can use to keep yourself and them on track.

What if my organization has different tools for one or more parts of a RAID log?

If you and your organization can get more value out of having one or more parts of your RAID log hosted somewhere outside your RAID log, then do it. Sometimes there are benefits if the tool is widely used. And, oftentimes, you won't have much choice. For example, if you are one of the rare PMs out there lucky enough to have an enterprise risk management tool, then tracking your risks in that tool rather than your RAID can help ensure your risks get the attention and governance needed.

However, you will find that for day-to-day management, it's more efficient to have the core parts of a RAID log in one place. Task switching between your RAID and outside apps consumes additional time and attention, which most busy project leader's cannot spare. You'll need to weigh the trade-offs of breaking up your RAID log into different apps.

What's the best way to see across the RAIDs of my team / portfolio / program?

Although managing a RAID in a spreadsheet is quick, portable and easy for individual project managers, it starts to become problematic when trying to aggregate data across all those RAID logs for a program or portfolio view. Aggregation can require manual copy/paste of critical RAID items, which is not at all practical. In case you are thinking of having everyone just work out of one massive RAID log spreadsheet, I can hopefully save you a lot of pain by recommending you never do that.

At some point in the growth of your organization, it will become too cumbersome to aggregate data from all your spreadsheet based RAID logs. This is when it may make sense to invest in a dedicated software product to do the job. There are Project and Portfolio Management (PPM) tools purpose-built for centralized project management and reporting. However, these tools generally do a poor job of RAID management, and are cost prohibitive for most organizations. In a pinch you can try task-based Work Management tools like Asana, Trello or Clickup. Having spent way too many hours of my life trying to get these tools to do the trick, I've found these miss the mark as well and aren't worth the hassle.

This is why the author of this book got together with some of his colleagues and started developing what they hope will be the ultimate RAID log solution: RAIDLOG.com. If your spreadsheet is working for you, then I cheer that. But, if you are looking for something more, I invite you to check out what we've put together at https://raidlog.com .

Case Study Conclusion: My friends in the UK

Let's go back to that stuffy little conference room in the UK midlands and pick up where we left off in this book's introduction.

The customer unloaded on us from their side of the conference table, taking turns venting their frustration. When they had exhausted themselves, I paused for a moment and asked, "Can you show me your RAID log?"

They looked at each other, then back at me. I let the silence go until it got quite awkward.

I looked up and down my team's side of the conference table. "Can you show me *your* RAID log?" My team had the same awkward, silent response. I didn't know if everyone in the room was embarrassed that they hadn't been using a RAID log, or if they were embarrassed that they didn't know what I was talking about. But, either way, my question had the intended effect.

I plugged my laptop into the conference room's overhead projector, opened a fresh clean RAID log and started at the top of the Issue log. "OK, let's review each of the current issues as you see them to make sure we understand them correctly." I had the customer walk through all of the issues in exhaustive detail, asking questions along the way and documenting it on the projected Issue log for all to see.

After a long, emotional review of the issues with the customer, I asked, "Is this all of the issues? Is there anything else to add?" It was a pretty long list by now, but I wanted to be sure I had it all. When they were satisfied that I had, I turned to my team, on this side of the table. "OK, how about you? What issues have you run into on this project which have kept you from being successful?"

Boom! They unloaded nearly as many issues caused by the customer as the customer had just listed about the team. Carefully facilitating the discussion, I let my team express their issues but kept it civil, all the while documenting everything in the Issue log. Many of these items seemed like very legitimate issues caused by the customer - the customer didn't have this or that ready, they weren't responsive, that kind of thing.

Once we had all the issues on the Issue log and we could all see them there together, it quickly became apparent that the root of most of our problems were missed and misunderstood *dependencies* between the project team and the customer. The project team needed quite a lot of information, material and support from the customer, but it was pretty clear that the customer had not understood those dependencies and their impacts.

Rather than focus on blame, I added a Dependencies log to my RAID log and had the project team walk through every one of their dependencies on the customer. As we added these to the Dependency log, we talked through each one with the customer to ensure they understood the dependency and why it was needed. We set a due date for each one and identified a responsible customer resource, and continued on to the next one.

What was magical was that by the afternoon of the first day, the mood had completely changed in the room. Instead of their side of the conference table vs our side, we had all gradually turned our chairs to face the RAID log projected on the wall; our new shared adversary.

In the days that followed, our teams worked very closely together, using our RAID log as the shared focus of our efforts and to track our progress. It wasn't us against them anymore, we were working together to overcome the issues we had jointly identified and agreed on - in the RAID log. We had taken the conflict between the customer and the project team and turned it into something concrete that we could understand and work on, together.

By the end of that week, the customer had retracted their legal notice of cancellation. Within 2 weeks, we had a new baseline plan agreed to. A few months later, we successfully delivered the project – using a RAID log.

APPENDIX: RAID LOG COLUMNS

There are a lot of different spreadsheet based RAID logs floating around the internet, and maybe around your organization. To give you some ideas on how to expand your RAID logs or to help you build your own from scratch, I've included this appendix of typical columns you can add to your RAID logs.

For each tab, I list the most commonly used columns, plus some optional extensions that might be useful in certain circumstances. Enjoy!

Risk Log

Below are the typical columns in the Risk log of a RAID log.

Column	Description
ID	Unique ID for tracking and reference
Title, in a "problem statement"	Use a problem statement form: as a result of <definite cause>, <uncertain event> may occur, which would lead to <effect on objectives>
State	State of the Risk. Usually a picklist denoting the lifecycle, including: • Raised (but still needs to be managed) • Open/Monitoring (response plan created) • Issue (the risk actually happened) • Closed (the risk no longer applies)
Description	Detailed description of the risk and its potential impacts and influencing factors
Date Raised	Date the risk was added to the log. This is good for tracking new vs old risks
Source	Source of the risk – the person who raised it or the forum it was raised in. This is handy when someone says, "where did this come from?"

Category	Categorization field for grouping risks for effective planning and management.
Probability of Occurrence	Numeric value representing the probability that the risk could happen. Can be a percentage, or a numerical scale (1-5)
Impact of Occurrence	Numeric value representing the impact of the risk, should it occur. You could use a monetary value, but assigning an accurate financial value can become quite involved, so it is usually more expedient to assign a numerical scale (1-5 or 1-100) with a definition of each level or a percentage.
P*I	Multiple Probability and Impact to arrive at a P*I score, or Risk Score which can be used to stack-rank your risks in order of importance.
Owner	The Owner is the person responsible for managing the risk. Most of the time, that will be the PM. But it could also be the technical lead, the Product Owner or Sponsor. The PM should keep on top of the Risk because they are accountable for the success of the project, but the Risk Owner is the one Responsible on the RACI.
Trigger Date	The date on which (or by-which) the risk would become an issue if it happens. After this date, the risk is immaterial.
Response	This is a text description of how you will respond to the risk.
Response Strategy	Picklist describing the strategy used to respond to the risk. This is optional if you have done a good job documenting the Response. It's more important to understand these options when documenting your detailed response than actually documenting the strategy. Picklist options are: • Avoid

- Mitigate
- Transfer
- Accept
- Escalate

Response Update	A text field with the latest update on the risk so you can see how your response is coming along. These can be timestamped entries or just the latest update
Date Updated	Date the last time the risk was reviewed or updated
Date Closed	Date the risk was closed or canceled
Reason Closed	Picklist or text describing the reason the risk was closed

- Risk passed the trigger date and did not occur
- Project ended
- Risk occurred and was converted to an Issue

Here are some additional columns that can be used to extend your Risk log in certain circumstances.

Column	Description
Contract / Charter Reference	Remember that any planning assumptions and constraints are inherently risks to your project if they don't hold true. So, adding those to your Risk log is a great way to start planning. This column is a reference back to the contract or planning documents, like the charter, where the assumption or constraint was documented. This can be handy if the risk turns into an issue as it can have contractual implications -for you, your suppliers or clients.

Impact Category	Some organizations like to be more specific with the Risk Impact and categorize risks by the constraints they may impact. Typical Impact Categories may include: • Scope • Schedule • Budget • Quality • Resource • Production operations
Date Proximity	Similar to the Trigger Date, many PMs like to measure the date proximity of a potential risk so they can focus more attention on those that are impending.
Escalations	If you need to create a paper-trail for who you escalated the risk to, when, and their response, then a special Escalations column can be useful.
Response Status	Red/Amber/Green indicator showing the status (on-track, at risk, off-track) of the risk response plan. When this is red, it means that the plan to mitigate the risk is going off track. This can be really useful for very critical risks.
Residual Probability	Residual probability is the probability the risk will occur AFTER the response strategy is implemented. It is typically more efficient to simply update the Probability of the risk after implementing your response, but sometimes it is nice to demonstrate the effective impact of your response, and thus the value of your risk planning
Residual Impact	Like Residual Probability, Residual Impact is the measure of expected impact after the response strategy. Like Residual Probability, it is more efficient to simply update the Risk Impact score after implementing these

measures, but it can be nice to break it out if you have to demonstrate the value of your risk planning.

Residual P*I	Residual Probability * Residual Impact
Residual Risk description	Explains what risk remains after your risk response is implemented. Even when Residual Probability and Impact are not used, it can be useful to describe what risk is remaining after your response actions, especially for more serious risks.
Financial cost of impact	Typically used only for the most impactful risks where EMV is used, this represents the total financial impact if the risk were to occur. If you use this field, then you should have an explanation ready for how you came up with this number.
Expected Monetary Value (EMV)	Probability as a percentage * Financial Cost of Impact. This represents the Expected Monetary Value of the risk, which can be useful for more advanced financial analysis.
Internal Only (team only) Flag	Flag indicating if this RAID item should be kept internal to your team. Instead of a flag, you can create data classification picklist of increasing sensitivity, such as "My-eyes only," "Internal Team Only," "Internal Org Only" or "All Stakeholders(default)" to allow for easy filtering

Action Items Log

Below are the typical columns in the Action Items log of a RAID log.

Column	Description
ID	Unique ID for tracking and reference
Brief task description, in the form of a "cause and effect statement"	We need to do x so we can get y
State	The state of the Action Item, usually a picklist denoting the lifecycle: • Open • In progress • Blocked • Completed
Status	Status (red/amber/green) of the RAID item, denoting whether it is on-track, at-risk or off-track.
Date Opened	Date the action item was added to the log. This is good for tracking new vs old items
Source	Source of the action – the person who raised it or the forum it was raised in. This is handy when someone says, "where did this come from?"
Owner	Person accountable for completing the action
Due Date	Date the task should be completed

| Comments/notes | Either a running log of the status or details about the activity |

Optional Extended Columns

Column	Description
Priority	Optional. I personally don't use this very often – date is enough of a driver. If you use L/M/H for priority, it's not long before everything is a High priority item.
Internal Only (team only) Flag	Flag indicating if this RAID item should be kept internal to your team. Instead of a flag, you can create data classification picklist of increasing sensitivity, such as "My-eyes only," "Internal Team Only," "Internal Org Only" or "All Stakeholders(default)" to allow for easy filtering

Issues Log

Below are the typical columns in the Issues log of a RAID log.

Column	Description
ID	Unique ID for tracking and reference
Title, in a "problem statement"	Use a problem statement form: This is wrong, causing this impact
State	Lifecycle state of the Issue. This will vary depending on your processes, but at minimum: • Raised • In action (or active) • Resolved pending root cause • Closed

Description	Detailed description, including any data related to cause.
Impact	Description of the impact of the issue. Be sure to clarify if issue impacts are limited to the project or extend to business operations
Category	Category - should match the categories of Risks
Owner	Person responsible for resolving the issue
Date Raised	Date the issue was identified and documented
Response Actions	A running log of actions and next steps in resolving the issue
Response Status	Status (red/amber/green) of the Issue response, denoting whether it is on-track, at-risk or off-track.
Date Resolved	Date the issue was resolved
Resolution	Summary description of the issue resolution
Remediation Actions	List of actions required to remediate the impacts

Optional Extended Columns

Column	Description
Escalations	If you need to create a paper-trail for who you escalated the issue to, when, and their response, then a special Escalations column can be useful
Stakeholders (Comm list)	List of stakeholders who need to receive communications regarding this open issue
Root Cause	Root cause of the issue. If you use this column, it may not be necessary for all issues, but may be a good idea for very impactful issues.

Internal Only (team only) Flag	Flag indicating if this RAID item should be kept internal to your team.
	Instead of a flag, you can create data classification picklist of increasing sensitivity, such as "My-eyes only," "Internal Team Only," "Internal Org Only" or "All Stakeholders(default)" to allow for easy filtering
Schedule Impact (duration)	The estimated impact to the duration of the critical path. If using this field, you should be able to summarize the total duration impact to critical path across all issues and this should match how late your project is
Cost Impact (amount)	The estimated cost impact of the issue. Ideally if you add up all the issues with cost impact, you arrive at something like the difference between your budgeted and actual cost.
Lessons Learned	Description of lessons that can be learned from this issue and applied to future projects to avoid similar problems

Decisions Log

Below are the typical columns in the Decisions log of a RAID log.

Column	Description
ID	Unique ID for tracking and reference
Decision to be made	Short title using cause and effect format: "Need to decide on X so that Y, otherwize Z."
State	Lifecycle state of the Decision. This will vary depending on your processes, but at minimum:
	• Raised

	• Pending Decision • Agreed
Status	Status (red/amber/green) of the RAID item, denoting whether it is on-track, at-risk or off-track.
Decision Needed by	Date decision needed in order to avoid impacts
Decision Maker(s)	Person or group responsible for making the decision
Impact	Description of the impact of the decision, including the impacts of NOT making a decision by the "needed by" date. Be sure to clarify if decision impacts are limited to the project or extend to other business areas
Impacted Stakeholders (to be informed)	Those impacted by the decision and how they are impacted. This is the list of stakeholders who must be informed about the result of the decision
Owner	Person responsible for following up with the Deciding parties to get the decision made
Decision Date	Date the decision was made and documented
Decision Made	Description of the decision that was made
Justification	Details about why the choice was selected in the decision. This is not strictly necessary but adds a lot of valuable insight into key project decisions and rationale

Optional Extended Columns

Column	Description
Decision Actions	List of the actions required to implement the results of the decision
Decision Options	List of the options available for the decision, and the benefits & drawback for each. This is difficult to track in a spreadsheet, but is worth documenting for key decisions.
Category	Where there are a large number of decisions to track across a large number of stakeholders, it can be useful to categorize the decisions
Decision Impacts	Describe any follow-on impacts of the decision. Some decisions can have negative impacts and may even result in your logging new risks or issues.
Decision requested by	Origination point for the decision request. This can be a person, a team, or an event like a meeting or workshop
Internal Only (team only) Flag	Flag indicating if this RAID item should be kept internal to your team. Instead of a flag, you can create data classification picklist of increasing sensitivity, such as "My-eyes only," "Internal Team Only," "Internal Org Only" or "All Stakeholders(default)" to allow for easy filtering

Lessons Learned Log

Below are the typical columns in the Lessons Learned log of a RAID log.

Column	Description
ID	Unique ID for tracking and reference
Title	Short title using cause and effect format: "We need to change X so that Y, otherwize Z."
State	State of the Lesson Learned, denoting the lifecycle. • Opened • In progress • Closed
Description	Detailed description o f the lesson, including a summary of the action needed to benefit from the lesson
Actions to take	Actions which need to be taken as a result of this lesson learned – to avoid repetition of issues or to take advantage of new findings or updated processes. Each action should have a name and a date on it
Related Items	Related issues, risks, deliverables, etc.
Category	Use one or more categories for the lesson – tying it to processes, services, products, customers, teams, etc.
Owner	Owner for ensuring all the lessons actions are completed
Lesson Update	Running log of updates for the lesson learned
Created by	Person who created the Lesson Learned
Created date	Date the lesson learned was created

Dependences Log

Below are the typical columns in the Dependencies log of a RAID log.

Column	Description
ID	Unique ID for tracking
Title	Short title using cause and effect format: "X needs Y to occur, otherwise Z will happen"
State	State of the dependency, denoting the lifecycle • Opened • Monitoring • Closed
Status	Status (red/amber/green) of the RAID item, denoting whether it is on-track, at-risk or off-track.
Impact if not delivered	Detailed description of impacts if the dependency is not met
Dependency type	Internal / external to your project's organization
Due date	The date the dependency must be met, otherwise there will be negative impacts
Owner	The person responsible for delivering the dependency
Dependency Update	Running log of updates of status and progress for the item

Change Log

Column	Description
Unique ID	Unique ID for tracking
Change Title	Short title using cause and effect format: "X is changing because of Y"
Change State	State of the risk, denoting its lifecycle. • Requested • In review • Rejected • Approved
Description	Detailed description of the change
Requestor	Who raised the change
Impacts of change	Summarize the impacts of the change, and of not making the change
Approver	List the people who must approve the change

Optional Extended Columns

Column	Description
Schedule impact	Quantified impact to project schedule
Budget impact	Quantified impact to project budget
Scope impact	Quantified impact to project scope
Resource Impact	Quantified impact to project resources
Quality impact	Quantified impact to project quality
Operational impact	Quantified impact to other business operations outside the project

Contact / Stakeholder List

Column	Description
Name	Contact Name
Organization	Contact Organization or Team
Org Role / title	Contact's job title and role within the organization
Project Role	Contact's role within the project
Email	Email
Phone	Phone

Time zone	Time zone of the contact, which is particularly useful when working internationally or with virtual teams
Notes	Text area for notes on the contact
Communication Preferences	Document any communication preferences. This can overlap with your communications plan and include what project related reports and notifications they should receive

About the Author

Kim Essendrup, PMP has been managing projects, programs and delivery organizations for over 20 years. He is one of the founders of Kolme Group, a project management consulting firm, CEO and co-founder of RAIDLOG.com, and he is co-host of the Project Management Happy Hour podcast, a PMI Authorized Training Partner (ATP).